Running 100 Miles
Part One

A History (1729-1960)

D1714475

Running 100 Miles
Part One

A History (1729-1960)

Davy Crockett

Utah Ultras LLC

Ultrarunning History Series

1. Frank Hart: The First Black Ultrarunning Star
2. Grand Canyon Rim to Rim History
3. Strange Running Tales: When Ultrarunning was a Reality Show
4. Running 100 Miles: Part One – A History (1729-1960)

Front cover: Sidney Hatch (1883-1966), in 1916, running 100 miles in a record time of 14:50:30 from Milwaukee, Wisconsin, to Chicago, Illinois. Photo taken by Chicago Daily News, Inc.

First Printing - Paperback

ISBN – 9798394978289

Ultrarunninghistory.com

Contents

"All the world is on the go, at the rate of one hundred miles in 24 hours. It looks as if people's legs are running or walking away with their brains."

— November 29, 1867, *The Fremont Weekly Journal*, Fremont, Ohio

Introduction

Running or walking 100 miles in one-go is an amazing accomplishment. Unfortunately, many people of today still mistakenly believe that a man without his horse invented the 100-miler in 1974, when he ran what he believed was 100 miles. Despite the false marketing claims that have circulated for decades, the history of running and walking 100-mile ultras on all surfaces, including trails, dates back centuries before 1974. More than 1,000 people had accomplished the sub-24-hour 100-miler before that famed **Gordy Ainsleigh** journey in the California Sierra in 1974 on the Western States Trail. Also, there were more than triple that number of people who reached 100 miles in under 30 hours in the many decades before.

In April 2020, *Runner's World* magazine erroneously called that 1974 solo run "The First 100-mile Ultra." It stated falsely, "the format that most of us know as 'ultrarunning' today (trail and road races, typically 50k to 100 miles) is barely 50 years old." Such statements are ignorant of the rich history of the past and the ultrarunners who paved the way, running ultradistances on dirt roads, tracks, and trails for more than two centuries.

By 1974, the 100-mile world record for men was 11:56:56 held by **Derek Kay** of South Africa. For the women, it was 21:04:00, held by **Miki Gorman** of California. If you erroneously think 100-mile ultras were invented in 1974 in California, you are deleting from the history of the sport many of the legendary 100-mile runners, including **Edward Payson Weston, Daniel O'Leary, Charles Rowell, Mary Marshall, Arthur Newton, Wally Hayward, Sidney Hatch, Hardy Ballington, Ron Hopcroft, Geraldine Watson, Miki Gorman**, and **Ted Corbitt**. This book will preserve their memories in the history of ultrarunning.

The Mile

The "mile" measurement has roots back to Roman times. The statute mile, a British incarnation in 1593, became adopted in the United Kingdom and later also by the United States. It should not be too surprising that walking and running, specifically the round number of 100 miles, came out of Great Britain and America. In other European nations, the meter and kilometer evolved during the 19th century as a standard unit of measurement. During the 20th century, the 100-kilometer distance (62 miles) became a far more popular ultra-distance worldwide to achieve and was much easier. But the 100-mile distance (161 kilometers) remained throughout the decades as a challenging milestone to achieve, especially in under 24 hours.

Yiannis Kouros, considered as the greatest ultrarunner of all time on tracks and roads prior to year 2000 or so, had a unique opinion that the 50 km, 50-mile and 100 km distances were too short to be considered ultrarunning. The 100-mile distance is significantly different for most runners because it requires night running, which he thought was an important challenge for a race to be considered an ultramarathon.

Very Early Ultradistances

The concept of walking or running extreme distances has taken place for thousands of years in many cultures, motivated mostly to relay swift communication between settlements or armies. Historic stories have been found regarding distances that were further than 100 miles, such as Pheidippides' run from Athens to Sparta in 490 B.C., a distance of about 153 miles.

In more recent centuries, aristocrats used "running footmen" to deliver letters. In 1728, it was reported that **Owen M'Mahon**, an Irish running footman, covered 112 miles in 21 hours running from Trillick to Dublin. Attempts to walk 1,000 miles in competition started as early as 1759 in England.

But what about achieving the round-number distance of 100 miles? When did the 100-mile quest begin and how did it grow?

CHAPTER ONE

The Early 100 Milers (1729-1874)

The earliest 100-milers were solo attempts that were motivated by wagers and usually required the person to achieve that distance in less than 24 hours. Accounts of a few early attempts were found in newspapers of the period. On September 11-12, 1829, **A. Higler**, of England, who was about 65 years old, accomplished the earliest known 100-mile attempt on a wager of 10 guineas. He walked back and forth on some ground along the side of the Thames River near Molesey Ferry, west of London. His bet was to accomplish the 100 miles within 30 hours, and he exceeded that, finishing in 28 hours.

In 1737, an unnamed journeyman carpenter attempted to walk 100 miles within 24 hours. They marked off a half-mile course from "Mother-Red-Caps" toward "Stamford Hill" on the road to Newington, England.

Many wagers were made. The carpenter struggled to finish in under 24 hours and missed it by just four minutes. It was reported, "However, the persons who imagined they had lost had the ground measured again and found there were three yards extra, which in the whole, amounts to 600 yards." The carpenter likely finished 100 miles in less than 24 hours, so they refunded the bets.

In 1758, a shoemaker from Shoreditch, England, agreed to walk 100 miles within 24 hours "and not to take any other nourishment but tobacco and water." Many wagers were made on the outcome. It is unknown whether he was successful.

In 1761, people were more impressed that a jackass traveled 100-miles in 24 hours carrying hardware and other items. That seemed like a much more practical accomplishment.

John Hague of Binns (Marsden), England, was the next

> 3. *Manchester, Aug.* 9. Friday last Mr. John Hague, of Binns, near Marsden, undertook, for a considerable Wager, to walk 100 Miles in 24 Hours, and performed the same in 23 Hours and 15 Minutes.

100-mile walker listed in history. For "a considerable wager," on August 9, 1762, Hague walked 100 miles on a Manchester Road in 23:15:00, proving that such a journey was possible in less than a day.

Women attempted 100 miles in those early years. In 1777, a shepherd's wife made the attempt to walk 100 miles on Newmarket Course in 24 hours. Huge amounts of money were wagered and, if successful, they promised the lady an annual salary for life, of 50l. The outcome is unknown.

Foster Powell (1734-1793) of London worked as a lawyer's clerk. He became perhaps the earliest notable pedestrian in 1764 when he walked 50 miles in seven hours on a wager. A few years later he walked 400 miles from London to York and back in five days, in 18 hours, bringing a focus on the idea of a six-day contest. He made this journey on a wager many times.

In 1786, Powell sought to walk 100 miles in less than 24 hours and succeeded in 23:45. He lowered his 100-mile time two years later, on July 20-21, 1788, to 21:20, walking on the Bath Road, between Box and London, England. The nation celebrated him as a celebrity, but he died in poverty. His death announcement in 1793

FOSTER POWELL.

2

included, "These extraordinary feats never produced him enough to keep him above the reach of indigence. Poverty, which he ought always to have kept a day's march behind him, was his constant companion in his travels through life, even to the hour of his death."

In 1789, a man walked 100 miles in 22:30 at Greenwich, England. "The ground was measured. He walked in a circle, which was an exact mile, 100 times round. He started at 4:00 in the afternoon Monday, walked all night, and went 100 miles by half past 2:00 on Tuesday. He did not appear much fatigued."

Also in 1789, a **Mr. Reid** ran 100 miles in 22:15 at Blackheath, England. "He would have done it less, had he not drank somewhat too much. During the performance he slept two hours and ran it in a measured circle of one mile, to the utter astonishment of all the spectators."

Captain Robert Barclay

Robert Barclay Allardice (1779-1854) or "Captain Barclay," of Ury, Scotland, was born to a Scottish family in 1779. His father had been a member of Parliament and owned extensive estates. When young Barclay was fifteen years old, he won a 100 guineas wager, walking heel-toe six miles in one hour, which at that time was considered a monumental accomplishment. When he was twenty years old, he covered 150 miles in two days.

Barclay is recognized in history as "the father of the 19th century sport of pedestrianism." He also was an officer in the army and thus called "Captain." His greatest long-lasting fame came from originating the "Barclay Match," walking one mile for 1,000 consecutive hours. Barclay took on many walking wagers and in 1806 he set his sights on the 100-mile distance. He completed the distance in 19 hours. His servant, **William Cross**, accompanied him and finished with the same time.

Other Early Sub-24-Hour 100 Milers in the British Isles

There were many other early 100-mile accomplishments in Great Britain and Ireland. Newspaper articles of the time preserved a few of them.

They were all conducted on dirt roads, and most were solo attempts attached to a wager. The accuracy of course measurements can be called into question, but because large wagers were usually involved, serious efforts were made for precise measurements.

Some of the many successful 100-milers in 24 hours are shared in this section to help the reader understand the sheer volume of these accomplishments. For every success, there were probably about 2-3 failed attempts too. We are left to wonder how many other efforts were never reported in the newspapers.

In 1810, **Edward Millen** (1781-), of Bethersden, Kent, England ran 100 miles in 23:25 on Charing-heath at Ashford, Kent, England. "Mr Millen performed the first eight miles in an hour and seven minutes and went a mile in eight or nine minutes for some time after. Toward the close, he appeared much fatigued, and his feet were swollen considerably."

Charing Heath

In 1811, **Mr. Oliver** walked 100 miles to London in 23:50, arriving "very lame, but overcame every obstacle, and did ten miles in the last two hours."

Royal Oak Inn, Wrotham

In May 1816, **Edward Millen** again attempted to run and walk 100 miles on a half-mile out-and-back section of a rough dirt turnpike road near Wrotham, England, with Royal Oak Inn being in the center. He started off running eight-minute-miles for the first thirteen, dined for 45 minutes and then continued. He then implemented a run/walk strategy for the rest of the way and finished in 23:54. "This feat may be considered as one of the most difficult executions, as the ground on which it was performed was very uneven, and it rained almost incessantly the whole 24 hours."

Also, that month in 1816, **George Wilson** (1766-1839), age 50, the "Blackheath Pedestrian," was a mega-mile pedestrian who put in many miles as a book peddler. He attempted a 100-mile walk in 24 hours on Hills Road near Cambridge, England, walking one mile out and returning. "In 24 hours, he failed by a quarter of a mile only, having performed 99 ¾ miles, when the time expired." Six months later, he successfully walked 1,000 miles in a record 17 days, 23:19:10. The local newspaper was not a fan of such feats. "If every idle fellow who chooses to take an extraordinary long walk is to be paid for his trouble, we should never have an end of such useless exertions, nor of the evils they bring on the indolent and thoughtless, who lose their time in witnessing them."

George Wilson

Miles.	Min.	Sec.	Miles.	Min.	Sec.
5	37	—	5	90	39
5	36	22	5	64	—
5	36	15	5	68	—
5	37	—	5	90	14
5	45	—	5	98	40
5	39	10	5	90	10
5	40	—	5	84	30
5	40	13	5	98	6
5	69	—	5	140	30
5	40	10	5	—	—

On June 30, 1817, **Mr. Yates** also came up a bit short. He was a yeoman from Mitcham. On a bet of 200 guineas, he wagered he could walk 100 miles in 24 hours. His course was a five-mile trail at Martin's Grove, on part of Epping Forest. He ran the first 50 miles in 7:10, but later was greatly affected by the heat and a strained leg, and had to stop at 95 miles in 20:45:40. "A re-measurement of the five miles turned out to be a full half mile short, arising from accident."

In 1820, a young farmer near Farnham, England, found 100-miler success and 20 guineas for his effort. He ran a five-mile stretch of Andover Road, reached 60 miles in 10:30, ate a good dinner and then continued. With only one mile left and two hours, his knee went lame. Somehow, he finished the 100 miles, limping in under 24 hours with four minutes to spare.

The 100-miler reached Cambridge in 1822 when a pedestrian walked a measured piece of ground on the green below Castle Mound. He finished in 23:50. "Immense crowds were on the spot during the whole of the time, and it is

Castle Mound

said the wager was fully and fairly won by the pedestrian, who is a small spare-looking young man."

In June 1822, **Moses Meredith**, "the Jewish Pedestrian," walked 100 miles in 24 hours at Hampstead Heath, "and finished his task with ease and could have won had he had two hours less time, as he had walked 95 miles by 21 hours."

Hampstead Heath

John Wright

Near misses were common. **John Wright** (1770-1844) was a 51-year-old tailor from Yorkshire, an army veteran who attempted 100-miles in 24 hours multiple times. In 1822, he made an attempt on a mile stretch of Romford Road between milestone five and six. "He failed in his task and lost his wager by three minutes and a half." Someone had run into him as victory seemed sure and injured his foot. He tried again the following month on Highgate Road, near the Highgate Archway in London, and this time finished in 23:37.

During May 1823, in Dublin, Ireland, a Scottish man, **Hugh Russell**, age 28, attempted to walk 100 miles in under 24 hours, doing laps around the Blessington Street Basin reservoir in the heart of Dublin for 100 sovereigns. "Although a man of low

Blessington Street Basin

stature, he performed the task in a quarter of an hour within the time." Two years later he made it even tougher on the race grand at Worcester. He walked 100 miles in 24 hours, pushing a wheelbarrow.

In September 1823, **Robert Skipper** (1789-1842) accomplished a 100-miler in 23:51 on a piece of ground on Pitchcroft, near Worcester, England. He worked as a "ostler" (took care of horses) at an Inn in Norwich, England and had also served in the army for up to 15 years. During his walk, he took plenty of rests. His moving time was 20:48. "He was escorted to the ground and back by a band of music, attended by an immense concourse of persons."

Robert Skipper

Even teenagers were successful. **John M'Mullen**, age 16, a slender boy from Cumberland, Ireland, walked 100 miles in 23:40 at Penrith, England, going from Mitre Inn to the New Brewery in March 1825. M'Mullen's mother was a tough pedestrian herself. When she was 60 years old, she walked twenty miles in 3:59 in London. "She accomplished the whole with apparent ease, to the surprise of the numerous spectators. She was wholly unprotected during her journey, and had to encounter many interruptions on the road, a great part of which is thickly inhabited." In 1830, it was claimed that she walked 100 miles in 23:50 at Ranelagh Gardens. If true (although doubtful) she was the first known woman in history to break 24 hours.

In 1827, another youth, age 18, reached the 100-mile milestone in 23:42 at Sudbury, England. And of course, there was the ridiculous. In 1827, **William Berecley**, age 17, of Inverness, Scotland, walked 100 miles in 24 hours alternating each mile, walking backwards, in Lane End, in the Potteries in London. "Although the weather and state of the road were much against him, he completed his task having an hour to spare."

In 1830, **Thomas West** also took on a wild task at Hoxton, England. Two hours before attempted 100 miles in 24 hours, he was to go through a brutal three-hour warmup: walk three miles forward, three backwards, run three miles, role a trundle hoop two miles, wheel a barrow two miles, pull a cart one mile, and pick up 100 stones placed one yard apart. He succeeded in the first task, and then barely missed 100 miles, reaching 98.5 miles in 24 hours.

Each year, for the next several years, there were many other successes reaching 100 miles in 24 hours. There were many mentions published in the English newspapers. The fascination of spectators in the small rural towns was amazing. "Anxious crowds awaited him near the time of his arrival at each town, cheering vociferously, as on the several occasions he neared the goal." In London, "Immense crowds were on the spot during the whole of the time." In Devon, England, "Anxious crowds awaited near the time of arrival at each town, cheering vociferously."

During that era, it also intrigued people that engineers were constructing steamships that could travel 100 miles in 24 hours as it steamed across the Atlantic Ocean. They were also amazed hearing that a man rode a horse 100 miles in 24 hours.

First 100-milers in America

In 1829, a correspondent of the *Richmond Enquirer*, reported that "an Osage Indian" in Arkansas could run 100 miles in 24 hours. In 1835, it was also reported that a Native American had covered 100 miles in a day, carrying a bar of lead weighing 60 pounds.

In October 1837, **Jacob M. Shiveley** (1786-1873) of Chambersburg, Pennsylvania, covered 100 miles in a day. He was referred to as "the great pedestrian." He was in competition against **David Webb**, who gave up at 79 miles. It was a very early 100-mile race between two people. Shiveley finished in 23:40:30. "He is a mechanic employed at Girard College, and was at work until noon of the day that he accomplished the undertaking. Although much fatigued at the expiration of the feat, he was heard to say that he should commence work again on Monday morning."

Another 100-mile race took place when **W. Jackson** "the American Deer" and **J. Brian** of London competed near Birmingham, England.

A typical 100-miler in the 1840s

What were these early solo 100-milers like? A detailed account was given for an August 1842 attempt conducted in Newry, Northern Ireland, by a 33-year-old Irishman named **M'Mullen**. (It is likely that he was the same **John M'Mullen** mentioned before who did 100-mile walks as a teen.) For his course, the ground was measured a half mile, starting at a place called the Watering

Richard Marks

8

Dam to the first turnpike on the Belfast Road. He would do a total of 100 out-and-backs on this half mile stretch. "Proper persons were appointed who were to give the pedestrian check tickets on his finishing each mile, so that there should be no question that he performed his voluntary task to the letter."

M'Mullen's journey started at 4 p.m. and he continued at a brisk pace for the first six hours when he was reported to be somewhat flushed. By 11 p.m. his spectator crowd thinned, and he appeared to be fresher in the cooler weather. By morning, he was fatigued, and his feet were in pain. Five blisters were cut off, and he kept going fast. At the 22-hour mark, he said he was "all safe." Four or five times during the day, he stopped for a few minutes at the grandstands, quite confident of his powers. Before the last mile, he stopped for six minutes and then completed an impressive finishing mile in eight and a half minutes. His finishing time is unknown, but he reached 100 miles within 24 hours. "He was loudly cheered on coming in. During the evening he walked through the town apparently not much fatigued." Two years later, he did a similar 100-mile walk in Dublin, Ireland, on a half-mile stretch that ascended and descended a hill. He was required to walk several of the miles backwards.

During the period from 1800 to 1867, it is estimated that at least 100 individuals achieved 100 miles in less than 24 hours in the British Isles. By about 1845, the serious British athletes lost their fascination with walking ultra distances and concentrated on running shorter distances fast. It would take 30 years before England again turned serious attention to ultrarunning, once they became convinced that American walkers had surpassed them.

Running 100 miles

A few early 100 miler athletes actually ran rather than walked the distance. **Edward Rayner** (1785-1852), "the Kentish Pedestrian" was born at Lenham, Kent, England. In 1819, he competed against **Foster Powell** in a match to go from Canterbury to London Bridge and back within 24 hours, a distance of 111 miles.

On April 14, 1824, Rayner again took up a 100-mile challenge at Biddenden, England, to attempt to reach the milestone in 18 hours, a quest that had been tried many times by others who had all failed. It was described to as "the greatest undertaking ever performed in England."

He started off at a "jog-trot" of about a ten-minute mile pace at 6 p.m. The road at first was very muddy because of a tremendous shower of rain and hail before the start. He kept up a steady pace, resting at intervals for refreshment, only about 2-3 minutes each time. At mile 59, he was attacked with a "slight sickness" and bets were offered 3-to-1 against him but refused. He continued with sickness until recovering at mile 68. He then finished at full speed "amidst the ringing of bells, waving of handkerchiefs, the band playing 'See the Conquering Hero Comes,' and other demonstrations of joy and congratulations." His time was 17:52, a 100-mile fastest known time that was not to be matched until 54 years later, in 1878.

On June 17, 1861, **Henry Howard**, a famous long-distance runner from Portsmouth, England, ran 100 miles in 18 hours at Brighton, England. Previously, in 1859, he had also accomplished running 83 miles in 12:25 in front of 4,000 people in London.

The Tarahumara 100-mile Race of 1867

During the 1800s, the American public was introduced to the Tarahumara, the ancient native Americans from hidden high Sierra canyons in Chihuahua, Mexico. Exploring expeditions visited these peculiar people who made their homes in hillside cliffs. Visitors quickly discovered that the people had amazing long-distance running abilities and could run down deer during the winter snows.

The true name for these people was the *Rarámuri,* thought to mean "the running people," although some Tarahumara have said it means "runner with the ball." The Spanish, not understanding their language, named them the "Tarahumara."

A very early rugged mountain trail 100-miler took place in 1867. *The New York Herald* reported that eight Tarahumara women competed in a 100-mile mountain trail race. The competition was between two rival Tarahumara villages that were about ten miles apart, Bocoyna and

Sisoguichi. Each village sent their four fastest women runners. The course was around an oblong mountain located somewhere between the two villages. The runners needed to run around it 14 times for a total distance of about 100 miles. They posted guards around the course to ensure fair competition. Crowds of people came from many villages to witness the event.

The 100-mile mountain race started at 6:35 a.m. "The whole bevy were off at the word go, amid the wildest excitement, and the betting commenced." After the first loop of about seven miles, five women were together in the lead. The only stops they made were  to accept prizes along the way, drink water or eat pinoli, "a simple gruel made of parched corn, ground and sweetened with sugar."

One woman who ran had given birth to a child just ten days earlier. Heavy betting took place. Horses, cattle, sheep, pigs, goats, cats, dogs and other items changed hands.

After about 92 miles, only three women were left in contention, but by the last lap, the lone contending runner from Sisoguichi had fallen off the pace. The two winners were from Bocoyna and were "received with the loudest shouts of joy by their townspeople." The women were reported to finish in well under 24 hours. At the finish, nearly everyone was "on the ground drunk."

Yes, the earliest known 100-mile mountain trail race was not the Western States 100, which was held 110 years later. The founders of that race had no understanding of running history because they were horse endurance riders. Thus, false marketing claims were perpetuated and evolved through the years that Western States 100 was the first 100-miler, and that the founders invented trail ultrarunning or all of ultrarunning.

Edward Payson Weston's 100 milers

Edward Payson Weston (1839-1929) can be credited for launching the pedestrian period of ultrarunning worldwide. Despite his perceived arrogance and bravado, he introduced the public to extreme distance running, which fascinated millions of people for more than 40 years.

Weston was born in Providence, Rhode Island on March 15, 1839. He was not particularly strong as a boy and took up walking to improve his health with exercise. As a teenager, he worked for a time in traveling circuses. He was athletic and won prizes in "wrestling, running, walking and leaping competitions." When he was 22, on a bet, he walked from Boston to Washington to witness the inauguration of **President Abraham Lincoln**, covering 453 miles in about 208 hours. In 1867, he walked from Portland, Maine, to Chicago, about 1,200 miles, in about 26 days. That walk brought him worldwide fame.

During that walk to Chicago on rugged dirt roads that we would have called trails today, Weston had his eye on completing at least one 100-mile segment in less than 24-hours. Prior to this walk, Weston had tried nine times to walk 100 miles in 24 hours and failed each time, once within only two miles. He could win $10,000 for his 1,200-mile walk. But if he didn't complete a 100-mile segment in one day, he would lose $6,000 of his winnings. They gave him five attempts along the way, but the best he could do was 91 miles. On that day, his feet were so badly swollen that he could not go any further that day. "His shoes were pulled off and his feet were sore and discolored."

Some claimed that Weston purposely failed, in league with those betting against him, and was told what to do by his backers as various side-bets were made. "Weston set out on his one-hundred-mile journey, does half of it with perfect ease, gaining time all the way and with no signs of fatigue. He makes three fourths of the journey still ahead of time and not suffering in the least, swings along the last part of the stretch at the rate of five miles and a half an hour, as fresh as a lark, and has but nine miles more to go with three hours and seven minutes to do it in, when the men who have him in charge declare that he can go no farther. Whoever heard of a man with badly swelled feet hopping along hour after hour at the rate he went."

Others later claimed that with a closer look at the distance that day, the 91 miles were actually 100 miles. Weston would complain bitterly about the distance when he finished his journey in Chicago.

The next year, 1868, Weston finally achieved his sub-24-hour 100 miler when he covered 103 miles in 23:28 during a walk from Erie, Pennsylvania, to Buffalo, New York on April 4th. "An immense crowd was in attendance in the afternoon to witness his arrival at the post office, having tramped through a heavy snowstorm and muddy roads. On his arrival, he was said to be 'looking as fresh as a lark.'"

Weston next attempted to walk 100 miles in less than 24 hours at Riverside Park in Boston on June 4, 1868, for $2,500. His prior attempts were always out on the road and open to skepticism. By walking a loop course, his effort could be witnessed. An enormous crowd of 5,000 people were present to watch, entertained by a brass band. But he managed to only reach 90.5 miles in 22:52 before giving up. He admitted that he was not in proper condition and that by the time he reached mile 27, he could not eat anything. He said he lost $3,500 valued at $71,000 today.

Other opportunities arose for Weston to take part in 100-mile match races against others for sizeable sums of money, but he did not finish several competitions. In 1868, Upstate New York became the center for the 100-miler in both Troy and Buffalo. In September 1868, on a half-mile track at Rensselear Park, a popular resort at that time in Troy, Weston lost to **Cornelius N. Payn** (1847-1914) of Albany, New York, blaming his failure on the circular track which he was not used to walking on. Payn finished in 23:23:08. Other 100-mile races involving multiple walkers were conducted on that same Troy track that year.

100-mile Frenzy Begins

Thanks to the news about **Edward Payson Weston**, starting in 1867, a 100-mile frenzy began in America that would last for a decade until six-day races became the preferred ultra-distance. During this ten-year period, hundreds would attempt the 100-mile distance. It was written, "All the world is on the go, at the rate of one hundred miles in 24 hours. It looks as if people's legs are running or walking away with their brains"

In January 1868, **Mark Grayson**, age 23, walked 100 miles in 23:06 on a track in Leavenworth, Kansas, and was said to look "a little fatigued." An article in Arizona marveled at the frenzy. "A Wisconsin walker did 100 miles in 24 hours and felt none the

Edward Payson Weston

worse of it. A Canadian named **Gordon** recently walked 100 miles without sleep or rest."

Australia got into the 100-mile frenzy in January 1867. A pedestrian called "**Tarrengower Novice**" completed the feat at the Red House in Northcote, Melbourne, Australia. He finished in 23:38.

At Cambridge in February 1868, there was a strange interruption of a 100-mile attempt. "A man who gave the name of **Taylor** undertook to walk at Cambridge. He commenced his feat in the presence of a large number of spectators, but Taylor was put to the blush by certain questions put to him by Detective Danby, who politely intimated to Taylor that the great feat for cogent reasons could not be proceeded with. Taylor at once took the hint and left Cambridge."

100-milers in Indoor Skating Rinks

By the end of 1868, some 100-mile races started to be conducted indoors in ice skating rinks. Race promoters realized they could charge for the admission of spectators and put on splendid shows to induce hundreds of spectators to come and watch the spectacle of these distance races going in circles. They engineered the structures to pull in cold, outside air along the ice surface, while retaining some warmer air above. More often, it resulted in slushy ice. Converting skating rinks into walking tracks proved to be successful venues.

Cornelius Payn quickly became a very prolific 100-miler, competing at the distance multiple times within just a few weeks. He was 22 years old, about 5 feet 8 inches tall, 123 pounds, and described as "a lithe, wiry, well-formed unassuming, intelligent young man." In November 1868, he took his efforts indoors during a cold month in Buffalo, New York, to the skating rink there. "The track was about three feet in width, covered with tanbark, and the foothold was not the best." He finished in 22:30, resting three and a half hours along the way. If the walkers could figure out how to reduce their stoppage time, they could bring down their times significantly.

Boston also opened its new skating rink in 1869 to the 100-milers. The rink was located on Tremont Street and boasted the ability to accommodate 5,000 people, including skaters and spectators. It was said to include "warm and comfortable rooms, where polite attendants could always be found to assist in putting on skates." They installed a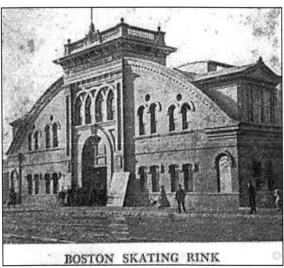

BOSTON SKATING RINK

restaurant, like a skybox, fronted entirely of glass that offered a "fine view of the ice surface, and of the entire audience." It was an amazing venue for a 100-mile match where **Young McEttrick** of Roxbury, Massachusetts, won a 100-mile race in 23:42:15, on May 25, 1869, during the Championship of New England. "He remarked that the only unpleasant effect produced by his long walk was a slight lameness caused by the action of the plank flooring upon which he walked." McEttrick's 100-mile best was 21:19:08, accomplished the previous year at Mystic Park in Medford, Massachusetts.

In 1868, New York City also opened its massive indoor "Empire Skating Rink," touted to be the largest rink in the country. It was 350 feet long, 170 feet wide, and 70 feet high. The ice bed was 200 by 130 feet. The structure included a raised platform for spectators and could seat 10,000 people, illuminated by 700 gas lights. At its grand opening, 3,000 skaters visited the rink. This venue was the site of many 100-mile competitions. Other skating rinks in Chicago, Illinois, Newark, New Jersey and Syracuse, New York, were used for 100-milers.

Empire Skating Rink

Horse Tracks Used for 100-Milers

Large outdoor horse track ovals were also used for 100-milers. During September 1869, **James L. Taylor** walked 100 miles in 23:26 at Lowell Riding Park at Lowell, Massachusetts. He came away in good condition with just a little soreness on the soles of his feet. He rested a total of 2:19 along the way.

Fast 100s

In October 1868, Weston walked 100 miles on a dirt road from Rye Station to White Plains, New York, and claimed to set a world best 100-mile walking time of 22:19:08, breaking a time made by **Laycock** at Troy, New York, September, 1868, of 22:59:54. However, they did not seem to be aware of McEttrick's recent time of 21:01:24. At the finish, a large crowd gathered around Weston, and he made a short victory speech. "The walk was made with little difficulty with no apparent ill effects afterward." Was it really a world best? Communication about records was of course, difficult in that era. **Edward Rayner's** 17:52 time set in 1824 was still the fastest known 100-mile time at that point. In more recent times, on March 23, 1867, **E. Thomas**, "The Northern Deer" was reported to walk 100 miles in less than 21 hours at the Royal Park Grounds in Blackburn, England.

The Back and Forth 1869 100-mile Race

Cornelius Payn was gaining fame and kept challenging **Edward Payson Weston** to races. On April 20, 1869, they competed in a back and forth 100-mile race on a rough, hilly dirt road/trail between Fredonia and Silver Creek, New York, a few miles from the shoreline of Lake Erie. They measured out a length of 12.5 miles. The two competitors would go back and forth four times to reach 100 miles. The winner would receive $250 from the citizens of Fredonia.

Before the start, Payn objected to the start in Fredonia, on a summit of a steep hill, and did not want to have to climb back up it over and over again. He also complained about the rainy day, which he felt would give Weston the advantage. Race officials overruled his objections.

On the given day, this historic 100-mile race began at 2 p.m. atop the challenging hill, in torrents of rain. Payn reached five miles in just 56:30. Weston reached that distance in an hour flat. It was reported, "All along the line of the road were scattered horse

Fredonia, New York

carriages filled with eager spectators, and each house poured out its last inmate to see the men go by."

Payn had a 23-minute lead when he completed the first 25-mile lap back at Fredonia with a total time of 4:59. The 100-mile race captivated the town. "Here the anxious ones were thronged in the street, in the windows of houses, and on the steps of the hotel. As the white cap of Payn came in sight, speculation began as to whether it was Payn or not, and when this became a certainty, many a jaw dropped."

But during the next 25-mile lap, Weston caught up and took the lead because Payn rested for 17 minutes. When Weston finished the second lap in 6:52, with a lead of 16 minutes, he was greeted with "tumultuous cheers." Payn and Weston greeted each other as the two passed by one another as Weston was early in his third lap.

They continued on through the night. On the last 25-mile lap, Weston rested for nine minutes and only had a seven-minute lead at mile 86. He looked exhausted when he reached Silver Lake at the turnaround, at 9:44 a.m. At mile 89, Payn caught up and went ahead because Weston was resting, laid out on a sofa in someone's house, covered in blankets at the 20-hour mark. He had been having chest pains and was examined by doctors who feared that he was having heart problems. They said it was "sure death" to attempt the remaining distance. Weston quit the race at that point. It was another Did Not Finish (DNF) against Payn.

Payn continued in terrible weather "with the wind throwing all it could at him in the form of sleet and rain." When he reached the 100-mile finish at Fredonia, the townsfolk were in disbelief that he had beaten Weston, who they thought was far superior. Payn still received cheers and finished in 22:52. Weston marveled at Payn's accomplishment on the difficult course, in the terrible weather.

Brutality in 100 Milers

Spectators of the early 100-milers watched with horror at times as trainers and backers would brutally force their athletes to continue, in order to win the enormous wagers. On one occasion in the Empire Skating Rink in 1870, **Edward Payson Weston** was attempting to walk 100 miles, but gave up. It was reported that toward the end, "he gave out entirely, whipped around the ring like a dog, to prevent his falling asleep from sheer exhaustion. Blood spirted from the severe lashing he received, and a whip was lashed on the tired legs that would no longer obey the exhausted nerve force of the failing pedestrian."

Reporters were horrified to see the number of spectators who came out hoping to watch the brutal spectacles. The exhibitions were compared to "people of old who caused their slaves to become purposely drunk in order to put on wretched displays in their intoxicated conditions."

Another reporter wrote in Buffalo, New York, which was a center of 100-miler interest, "The laws of this State prohibit cruelty to animals, yet the worst torture that can be inflicted on dumb brutes can scarcely equal that involved in a worse than useless walking match. Though self-imposed, the task ceases to be voluntary when once entered upon. Trainers and backers will hear no complaints while physical power holds out, but drive their victims about the track by a spur quite as effective and cruel as could be applied to a horse. It is brutality of the worst sort. Its result must be a lot of broken-down men, many of whom will doubtless find refuge ultimately in alms-houses."

Buffalo, New York

In 1871, Weston was again competing in a 100-mile match. It was reported, "The account of this achievement shows Weston to be a great donkey. On his ninety-third mile he got sleepy and had to be cow-hided and have ice clamped to his head by his friends to keep him awake. Lemonade, beef tea and tonics were poured down his throat to keep him to time. He suffered terribly but held on. His pallid face, set teeth, blood-dilated nostrils, showed his distress. The men yelled, and the women cackled at him encouragingly. Ammonia and whisky carried him through the last mile when he caved. Queer way, this, to make a living."

Early Women 100-milers

As early as 1777, women attempted to walk 100 miles in 24 hours. That year, a shepherd's wife accepted a wager and started out on a course at Newmarket, England. A rich lady promised that if she succeeded, she would receive a salary for life of 50 guinea per year. It is unknown if the shepherd's wife was successful.

Mrs. Harry Thomas

Writers in the newspapers were frequently rude when it was reported that a woman was trying to walk 100 miles. When **Mrs. Harry Thomas** attempted 100 miles in 24 hours in 1868, near St. Louis, Missouri, it was written, "The remarkable feature of the performance was that the dame was not to talk." They would also comment on their appearance. "Mrs. Thomas is a rather small built woman and would be considered rather good looking. She does not look to be very strongly made, nor capable of the fatigue of such a journey."

Thomas performed her walk in Concordia Park. A broad plank was laid on a trestle or framework on which she walked back and forth. "Quite a large crowd of spectators assembled at the park to see the start. With an elastic, buoyant step, Mrs. Thomas began her tedious march at 1 p.m." By night, she had slowed but continued without complaint. "Watchers were left with her and furnished her with the refreshments required and kept a record of the time and distance as each hour rolled by."

By morning, she looked very fresh, although her legs had swelled up and her steps were slower. At 23.5 hours she reached mile 92. "It being fully apparent that the remaining eight miles could not be made up in the concluding half hour, she ceased her walking amid the cheers and compliments of all bystanders." She vowed to try again in a few weeks.

Madame Moore – First Woman's sub-24-hour 100-Miler

A woman joined in the 100-mile frenzy that was taking place in America. **Anne Fitzgibbons**, a.k.a. **"Madame Moore,"** age 22, was a female pedestrian, clogger, and actress from England who had accomplished the "Barclay Match" of walking 1,000 miles in 1,000 consecutive hours at Manchester, England.

In 1868, she was being trained by **Cornelius Payn's** trainer for a walking match at the Rensselaer Park in Troy, New York. The male press was not impressed and criticized her for wearing "male attire." She soon walked 50 miles in 10:15:25 and then had her sights on 100 miles in 24 hours.

In November 1868, she walked 50 **Womɑn Pedestrian in Mɑle Attire.** miles in 9:50 in a Syracuse New York skating rink. Soon after, she was arrested on the streets in Rochester, New York, for being dressed in men's clothes and was "gobbled up by the police."

It was reported, "She came into court to settle damages. She stated that she had been engaged in the walking business for six months, and this was the first time she had been arrested. She said all her dresses were in a trunk at Troy, New York, and she had no change with her. The Squire told her she would be supplied with a dress at the penitentiary, where he would send her for sixty days. She wore blue pantaloons and vest, checked shirt, sack coat, jockey hat, and her neck was tastily dressed with a stand-up paper collar and fashionable necktie. Her hair was cut short and combed behind her ears."

She boasted at her court hearing that she could beat **Edward Payson Weston** in a race. At her sentencing, she agreed to reform, and her sentence was suspended. A month later she was in Buffalo, New York, the city that was friendly to walking matches. She was licensed by city officials to wear male attire during her exhibitions.

A couple months later, it was announced that Moore had died in Chittenango, New York, "from the result of over-exercise." The press seemed to delight at the news, commenting on her disgusting male attire and that she had hung out with "bad company."

However, a correction was quickly published, "We are happy to state she is yet in the land of the living, and astonishing the good people of Oneida, New York, with exhibitions of tall walking."

In March 1869, Moore walked 100 miles in 24 hours at the Concert Hall in the town of Oneida, New York. She was the first known woman to accomplish this. She walked the last mile in a speedy eight minutes. It was claimed that her actual walking time, not including rests, was an astonishing 21:30. There were

Main Street, Oneida, N. Y.

plenty of male skeptics. "Many are of the opinion that the miles were short ones, but be that as it may, the madame has demonstrated conclusively that she is no ordinary 'walkist.'"

The next month, in April 1869, Moore again walked 100 miles inside a hall in West Troy, New York. with a time of 24 hours. "She knocked down a West Troy man who insisted on accompanying her in her perambulations. The Madame's fighting weight is 150 pounds." Moore soon issued challenges to Weston and any other man to a 100-mile race.

Weston in the Empire Skating Rink

In May 1870, **Edward Payson Weston** attempted to walk 100 miles in under 22 hours inside the massive Empire Skating Rink in New York City. Many people were still skeptical of his abilities and thought he was a fraud. **W. W. Wallace**, the proprietor of the rink, wanted the city to make up their own minds and invited Weston to perform in front of an immense crowd.

Weston in Empire Skating Rink

The track laid out for him was three feet four inches wide in a circuit of 735 feet, requiring 717+ loops to reach 100 miles. Seven men served as judges in shifts. Weston was very confident and said he would accomplish his 100-mile task or "die in the attempt." He reached 50 miles in 10:35, on target, and finished in 21:38:15, making only nine stops, all less than ten minutes.

More than 5,000 spectators witnessed his finish. "The announcement of the result was the signal of a deafening burst of applause from the thousands who had assembled to witness the successful termination of the greatest pedestrian feat ever attempted. Mr. Weston did not seem in the least fatigued, stepping off as briskly on the last mile as on the first, and after the one hundredth mile had been accomplished, he addressed the crowd from the judge's stand, saying that it was love, not money, which had induced him to attempt the feat which he had just accomplished. It was his desire to free himself from the reputation which had been given to him by some of the daily papers of this city of being a 'humbug,' and to set right before the public, those who had befriended and defended him."

For Weston, there still were doubts about his 100-mile abilities. A man by the name of **James Smith**, claiming that he was the true champion pedestrian of America, charged that Weston's track was measured wrong, using the center of his lane. Because Weston hugged the inside of the lane on the turns, he clipped off two yards for every turn. Smith wrote, "Now I want to let the public to see that this man, as a walker, is a fraud and an

EDWARD PAYSON WESTON

impostor." He challenged Weston to a 100-mile race for a $1,500 prize and he said he would give Weston a five-mile head start.

That match never happened, but a year later, Weston again competed in the skating rink and reached 100 miles in 21:01. In 1873, Smith did finish 100 miles in 22:33 at Belle City Hall in Wisconsin. He falsely claimed that his 100-mile time was the fastest time ever accomplished.

Entertainment During 100-milers

With more crowds attending the 100-milers, walkers made more efforts to put on a show. In 1875, **Morrison** from Portsmouth, New Hampshire, walked 100 miles in Bangor, Maine. He finished in 23:55. A reporter wrote, "He walked the last mile backward, thus making an ass of himself."

Bands frequently were at the 100-mile races. When **Professor Sweet** walked 100 miles in 22:57 in New Haven, Connecticut in 1868, "during the last half hour the band accompanied Mr. Sweet about the track, playing lively music to keep his spirits up, and sherry with eggs were given him for the same purpose."

The genuine attraction to watch 100-milers was to view a reality show of pain. "Instead of being like the ball match or even the horse race, it becomes a trial of physical powers, like the prize-fight, in which the agony of the participants forms the chief attraction to the public." Many thought that watching these painful spectacles would have absolutely no influence in encouraging "a sedentary and well-fed population to take to their legs for exercise."

Continued 100-mile Frenzy

By the mid-1870s, the 100-mile frenzy was still in full operation in America. More and more walkers took up challenges to reach the milestone. It is estimated that by 1875, more than 150 people, both professional and amateur, had accomplished the sub-24-hour 100-miler in races or solo challenges. The 100-mile frenzy would get even more intense in the coming years.

Note that these very early sub-24-hour walkers were not technically racewalker "Centurions." That classification which came to be in 1911, was only for amateurs, and they had to do the walk with strict racewalking rules in judged events. Most of these very early 100-mile walkers in the 1870s just walked free-form.

CHAPTER TWO

100-Milers 1874-1878

Mark Twain's 100-miler

Samuel Clemens "Mark Twain" (1835-1910) joined in the 100-mile craze. He attempted to walk 100 miles from Hartford, Connecticut, to Boston, Massachusetts, in two days with his pastor, **Joseph Hopkins Twitchell** (1838-1918). The two had taken many ten-mile walks together to enjoy social chat and exchange views. They would always return home from these walks with "jaw ache" but were never foot sore. So, they hoped to walk all the way to Boston to store up enough "jaw" to last them through the winter.

The two started on November 19, 1874, at 9 a.m. intending to stay on an old turnpike, to see the hamlets along the way, and avoid walking on the railroads. After ten hours and 28 miles, they stopped for the night. "Before retiring, they had a consultation and decided that their undertaking had developed into anything but a pleasure trip and was actually hard work." They decided to postpone their pedestrian tour for a year or so.

In the morning, they walked seven more miles for a total of 35 miles, and then took the train to Boston. Twain said, "My knee was so

Mark Twain

stiff that it was like walking on stilts." It was written, "Mark Twain wishes it to be distinctly understood that the walk was not a failure, and they would have continued the trip had Mr. Twitchell not have been under engagement to preach in Newton on Sunday morning." He said that next time he would reserve a week for the 100 miles but that he was not anxious to take away **Edward Payson Weston's** laurels because he did consider that he was at least as good as Weston.

Daniel O'Leary

In 1874, **Daniel O'Leary** (1841-1933) came into the 100-mile scene, stealing away much of the spotlight that had been on **Edward Payson Weston** (1839-1929), eventually becoming the top American pedestrian. O'Leary was born in Ireland and, as a child, lived through terrible years of potato blight, causing horrible starvation and disease. In 1866, like so many other Irish, he immigrated to America. He could not find work in New York City, so he settled in Chicago, worked in a lumber yard and sold books door-to-door. He built up his endurance from speed walking his routes.

Daniel O'Leary

In 1874, O'Leary overheard a group discussing Weston's attempts to walk 100 miles in twenty-four hours. One person said that only a Yankee could accomplish the feat. Another commented that Weston was planning a trip to Europe. O'Leary said, "If he dropped into Ireland on the way, he'd get beaten so bad that he'd never again call himself a walker." Everyone laughed at him. He finally said that he thought he could beat Weston. They then roared with laughter.

O'Leary wanted to prove that an Irishman could also be a successful distance walker. He rented the West Side Rink on the corner of Randolf and Ada Streets in Chicago and announced that he would attempt to walk 100 miles in 24 hours. For training, he accomplished 70 miles in one day on a rough road.

O'Leary's First 100-mile Attempts

Mr. O'Leary Will Try to Walk 100 Miles in 24 Hours.

O'Leary made his 100-mile try on July 14, 1874. Most of the bets were against his success. At the start "he was greeted with a hearty round of cheering." He did not dress up as other pedestrians of the time did, and simply wore a white woolen shirt and dark pants. Six judges took part, along with two scorekeepers. It was reported, "The area of the rink, which was scientifically surveyed, is 400 feet. Thirteen and one-fifth circuits make up a mile, and sixty-six circuits comprise five miles."

O'Leary began at 8:35 p.m. His first five miles took 65 minutes and he then sped up. At 15 miles, he was described as having "the air of a man who was determined to conquer or die."

His fuel during the walk was only ice water and brandy. The summer heat inside the rink was terrible, and the track was rickety, but O'Leary succeeded and finished in 23:17. It was more than two hours slower than Weston's best, but he proved an Irishman could walk 100 miles in less than 24 hours.

A month later, O'Leary tried again, this time to reach 105 miles in 24 hours for a

O'Leary, the Pedestrian, Accomplishes His Undertaking.

wager of $1,000. The track he walked on was wet and slippery because of a leaky roof, but they threw down a little sawdust to make the walking surface better. O'Leary walked with an injury, a swollen hand, caused by being bitten recently by a pet monkey.

He began his walk at 10 p.m. and started out walking 9 to 11-minute miles. Various guests, including a police officer, walked with him at times, but had difficulty keeping up. In the end, he reached 105 miles in 23:17. Some contended that he had not walked some of the corners fairly. To put away the doubts, he walked another mile, reaching 106 miles in 23:27:13. "At the conclusion of this feat, O'Leary was rubbed down with alcohol and expressed his willingness to walk 110 miles within the twenty-four hours whenever the inducements offered called for exertion. During the evening, a purse was collected for the plucky pedestrian."

O'Leary challenged Weston to a 250-mile walking match but was brushed off by Weston who said, "Make a good record first and meet me after."

Tit for Tat – O'Leary vs. Weston

To further prove that he was better than Weston, O'Leary wanted to beat Weston's best time for 115 miles and "leave him in the shadows." At Philadelphia, he succeeded, reaching 115 miles in 22:59, beating Weston's best time by an hour. He should have continued to do more miles within 24 hours for a record, but he did not.

Weston noticed, and a couple weeks later in May 1875, he made an attempt in New York to reach 118 miles within 24 hours. He came up one mile short, reaching 117 miles, but reached 100 miles in 20:01:58 "without a rest." He was pleased that he beat O'Leary's 115 miles at Philadelphia.

1875 100-mile Races

During 1875, there were more than 20 successes by pedestrians in reaching 100 miles in 24 hours. Some of those achievements occurred in races. Nearly all of them were conducted indoors in front of paying spectators.

On April 10, 1875, O'Leary raced 100-miles at the American Institute Hall (formerly the Empire State Rink), at the corner of 63rd Street and 3rd Avenue in New York City. He competed against **John L. DeWitt** (1839-1889) of Auburn, New York and gave DeWitt and 10-mile head start. The purse for the event was $1,000. DeWitt gave up after 57 miles and O'Leary finished his 100 miles in 23:52:14.

O'Leary raced 100 miles again in October 1875 in his familiar Chicago West Side Rink. He competed against pedestrian **John T. Ennis** (1842-1829), another Irish-American from Chicago, for $500. Ennis was to walk 90 miles to O'Leary's 100 miles to win the prize. At O'Leary's 50-mile mark, achieved in 8:52:18, Ennis  was four miles behind. Ennis walked at a steady gait, but he quit at 67 miles. O'Leary finished 100 miles in a staggering 18:53:43, a walking 100-mile world record. "A considerable attendance witnessed the close of the walk, and much enthusiasm was manifested." But O'Leary's walking 100-mile time was more than an hour slower than **Edward Rayner's** fastest known 100-mile time in 1824, when he ran 100 miles in 17:52.

O'Leary Beats Weston Head-to-Head

Weston's most famous achievement at that point was reaching 500 miles within six days in December 1874, which kicked off the six-day race era that lasted for more than thirty years. The history of the six-day races will be covered in another book.

In November 1875, O'Leary and Weston finally competed head-to-head in a

O'Leary and Weston

six-day walking match held at the Exposition Building in Chicago. O'Leary reached 100 miles in the lead at 20:48:21 and defeated Weston by 51 miles, reaching 500 miles in 143:13, and finishing with 503 miles. Both became very rich men, dividing the $11,000 gate money evenly. That was worth more than a quarter million dollars in today's value.

Pedestrian Fever in Chicago

O'Leary's fame spread through Chicago as pedestrian fever caught fire across the city. "It has wholly transformed the appearance of the streets. The

PEDESTRIANISM.

Result of O'Leary's Success on the Residents of This City.

sidewalks are now crowded with hurrying pedestrians all stepping forward, male and female, in true professional style, with heads thrown back and hands held up high, each apparently striving to achieve a six-mile gait. Street cars pass along once in a while, but if they contain any passengers at all, they are cripples, weak and infirm old people, or shop boys with heavy bundles. Men can be seen with watches in their hands timing themselves as they dart forward, and muttering strange words about minutes, seconds, and distances."

100-mile race busts

Many of the early 100-mile races were busts, with no one finishing. Often races were stopped once there was only one man left standing. In 1875, a 100-mile race was billed as the "Championship of America." It was held at the American Institute Hall in New York City. The competitors were **George B. Coyle** (1837-1917), the champion from Wisconsin, and **William Edgar Harding** (1848-1912) of New York City. "Great

AMERICAN INSTITUTE HALL, 1879 THIRD AVENUE, BETWEEN 63D AND 64TH STREETS.

interest was manifested in the match." Coyle was the favorite because Harding had never walked in a match of more than 50 miles.

The highly anticipated race was held on May 28, 1875, starting at 10:37 p.m. Both walked non-stop for about the first 35 miles, with Harding in the lead. It still was close when they reached 50 miles in about 11:30. "The exertion and fatigue were visible on both men, although Harding made an occasional spurt, which won the applause of the large audience present during most of the day." But later in the morning, Coyle suffered terribly. "His limbs were chafed, felt sore, and a pain in the stomach and groin caused him intense agony." He quit at mile 75. Instead of finishing the race, Harding was declared the winner, reaching 78 miles in about 24 hours.

Mechanics Hall, Boston

Another 100-mile race was a bust in Mechanics' Hall in Boston held May 3, 1875, between **George F. Avery** (1854-1885) of Maine and Massachusetts and **Charles A. Cushing**, (1847-1920) of Boston. Cushing reached 96 miles and Avery 84 with a cut-off time of 24 hours.

In December 1878 "The Great 100-mile Walking Match," was held in Belvidere, Illinois between **Donahue** and **Cross** at Union Hall. "It didn't amount to much. They walked about 35 miles apiece and quit. The thing was also a failure financially."

One-hundred-mile races were often held outdoors on horse racing tracks. In Jun 1875, a 100-mile race billed as "the Championship of New England" was held outdoors at Mystic Park, a horse track in Boston, Massachusetts. The competitors were between an Englishman, **John Haydock** of New York, and Bostonians **George F. Avery**, and **Charles A. Cushing**. Haydock won in 23:36:29. Cushing dropped out at 71 miles, and Avery at mile 75. Haydock won $300.

Weston in England

In 1876, the world-famous pedestrian, **Edward Payson Weston**, age 37, traveled to England to compete against any British walker. His trip had a significant impact on the history of ultrarunning because it stirred up pedestrian fever in that country. The British press wrote, "At last Englishmen have had the opportunity of judging for themselves the capabilities of American walkers." They were skeptical about Weston's achievements and doubted that he could reproduce his efforts in England. "Englishmen have refused to accept without some confirmation of the accounts of long journeys traversed by Yankee peds. Edward Payson Weston has arrived in England at an opportune moment to convince the skeptical and satisfy the curious. No English aspirant for pedestrian honours ever came before the public with such flourish and trumpets." Weston was determined to prove his British skeptics wrong.

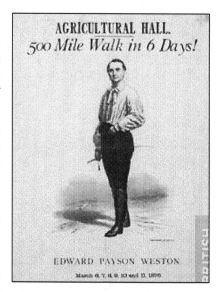

24-hours Against William Perkins

For his first English race, Weston competed against **William T. Perkins**, "the champion pedestrian of England," in a 24-hour competition at the Agricultural Hall in Islington, London, England on February 8, 1876. Perkins was "the wonder of the day among English walkers – The Champion, beyond all doubt at any distance up to fifty miles." He was known as the only man who had ever walked eight miles within an hour.

Perkins was no match for Weston's walking experience and endurance. He quit after only 65 miles because of blisters. His socks were saturated with blood and had to be cut off his swollen feet. The press still thought he was a hero. "Perkins, though broke down, proved himself to be what all who know him have long thought of him – game to the backbone."

Weston continued on alone and suffered through a period of vertigo and pain. He fueled on beef tea, beaten-up eggs, toast, jelly, grapes, prunes, coffee, tea, milk sugar and diluted brandy. As he neared 100 miles, he increased his pace "amidst the most enthusiastic cheers at his pluck and determination." He hit 100 miles in 19:20 and reached 109 miles in 24 hours. He caught the attention of the British and published a challenge to any man in England. 100-mile walking during that era in Great Britain was not very widely competed at that time, but the Brits started to train furiously.

48-hours Against Clark

A week later, Weston defeated **Alexander Clark** of Hackney, England, in a 48-hour walk. Early on, the race was close and competitive, but Clark quit after 55 miles and Weston reach 100 miles in 23:30:35, and then showed off by walking a lap backwards. He went on to reach 180 miles in 48 hours.

Weston's Dominance in England

Weston's early dominance at ultra-distances in England was an embarrassment to English sports authorities. Some tried to dismiss it. "Nothing is more common than to hear opinions expressed to the effect that the recent performances of Mr. **Edward Payson Weston**, however marvelous they may be, are of no practical utility."

Next, the English wanted to see if an experienced runner could defeat Weston. **Charles Rowell** (1852–1909), was allowed to run or walk as he pleased in a 75-hour competition against Weston, and Weston spotted him 50 miles ahead. Rowell quit after 176 miles and Weston reached 275 miles.

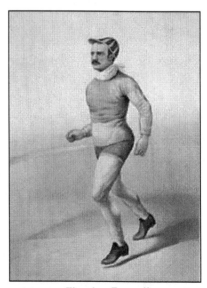

Charles Rowell

Weston continued to compete in England in many distances greater than 100 miles. By May, the competition became greater, as several Brits were able to walk sub-19-hour 100-milers in Agricultural Hall in larger races. **Daniel O'Leary** joined in competing internationally when he also went to England in 1877, beating Weston again in a head-to-head six-day race. The English were stunned at the dominance of Weston and O'Leary over the best of England. They were determined to catch up and regain their top spot in the world in long-distance running.

100 milers in America

100-mile accomplishments continued back in America, including the first known walker from California, when **Robert Allen** reached the milestone in 24 hours at San Jose, in September 1876.

At Racine, Wisconsin, **James Smith** succeeded in walking 100 miles in 22:33 in January 1874. He walked in the Bell City Hall where the track was carefully measured. The organizers hired judges and time-keepers. During his walk, he only ate chicken. "His feet and legs were terribly swollen. Round and round he went, varying his gait, and at times it was painful to see him, but he still kept on doing off his miles on an average of about 15 minutes."

O'Leary vs Ennis

The *Chicago Times* wrote, "Ever since **Dan O'Leary** began his career as a pedestrian, he has been fighting down men who believed that because they were of his city of Chicago, that they were as good as he. The most promising of these men had been **John Ennis**, who had been a prominent athlete."

On November 10, 1877, O'Leary and **John T. Ennis** (1842-1829) faced off in a 100-mile race. It was held at the Exposition Building in Chicago for $500. There were hopes that one of the athletes would break 19 hours.

A large crowd of spectators cheered the start, but soon afterward, violent pain in Ennis'

John Ennis

bowels attacked him and for some time, people feared he would have to quit very early. But he continued on, using spurts of speed. By mile 46, O'Leary already had a 15-mile lead and Ennis was still suffering. "At the end, O'Leary was fresh as a daisy, while Ennis was pumped out, done-for, busted, ruined, and gone." Ennis only reached 54 miles. Despite the lack of competition, O'Leary went on and finished 100 miles in 19:59:40.

Go As You Please – Running Allowed

1878 was the year when the six-day race started to take the spotlight away from the 100-mile race because there were larger winnings possible. **P.T. Barnum** (1810-1891), of circus fame, held the first formal six-day race in 1875 at his Hippodrome in New York City, but the six-day really took off in 1878 when they established the Astley Belt race series. The first edition of this international race was held in the Agricultural Hall in London, England. The British wanted to level the playing field against the Americans and introduced "Go as you please" rules to the sport, allowing running. This simplified officiating and reduced protests about rule-breaking because of walking form.

For years, debates occurred about running vs. walking. Back in 1873, it was written, "Pedestrianism is divided into two heads, running and walking. Where walking ends and running begins, no one has yet been able to determine. Men walk at the rate of eleven miles and a half in an hour without being either cautioned or disqualified. Running amok means getting in front of an opponent on a muddy day and splashing him as much as possible, a favorite performance of the limit men in amateur handicaps."

Pedestrian historian, **P. S. Marshall** explained, "Competitors would be able to 'walk, trot, run, mix, lift or introduce a new style of pedestrianism if clever enough.' This was a decision made for two reasons, one of which was apparently because of Weston's 'wobbling gait' which was considered as not being textbook heel-and-toe, and the other was because there was a view that because the American athletes were so much better at walking than their British counterparts, a method of progression was needed to be invented to disadvantage the best of those athletes."

Daniel O'Leary won the First Astley Belt Six-Day Race, held in the Agricultural Hall, reaching 520 miles, beating 17 other competitors.

100-mile Record Broken

In 1878, thanks to "go as you please" rules, well over one hundred athletes successfully completed races of at least 100 miles, with times that fell dramatically as they learned to trot.

As more British long-distance runners extended their endurance to ultra-distances, they began to truly excel at distances of 100-miles and greater. The Agricultural Hall in London became the premier ultrarunning venue for the world in 1878. As "go as you please" rules were adopted, speed increased as the athletes learned how to incorporate trotting along with their walking. Several British runners started to reduce their 100-mile times close to 18 hours. The long-standing 1824 100-mile record of 17:52 set by **Edward Rayner** of England was then 54 years old. No one else had

Agricultural Hall

reached 100 miles in less than 18 hours, not until 1878.

A "Long Distance Championship of England" was held at the end of October 1878 in the Agricultural Hall in the form of a six-day race with 23 runners. About 10,000 spectators were on hand when **Henry "Blower" Brown** (1843-1900), of Fulham, England, broke the 18-hour barrier reaching 100-miles in a split-time of 17:54:05. Eight runners that day reached 100 miles in less than 24 hours.

Blower Brown

GEORGE HAZAEL.

A day after that six-day race finished, another historic six-day race began, also in the Agricultural Hall. It was for "second class" men who had been excluded from the championship race the week before. **George Hazael** (1845-1911) from London, England, was in the field and certainly had a chip on his shoulder being left out of the main event a week earlier. He was a "celebrated" long-distance runner and had beaten some of the best runners in England at distances up to 12 miles. He began competing in ultra-distance races in 1877 and quickly excelled.

At the start, Hazael shot off into the lead and kept increasing his lead during the day. He surprised everyone when he broke **Edward Rayner's** 54-year-old 100-mile world record with a time of 17:03:06 and went on to win the six-day race with 403 miles.

Hugh Lowther (1857-1944) was the son of the Earl of Lonsdale in England but viewed by some as being irresponsible. When he was 21 years old, he took part in a bet of five guineas to take part in a road race of about 100 miles held in June 1878, from Knightsbridge Barracks to the Ram Jam pub on the Great North Road. He finished in an uncertified 17:21, nine minutes shy of Hazael's recent world record. The £5 bet he won was nothing compared to the satisfaction of trouncing his rivals. He would later inherit a fortune and

become the 5th Earl of Lonsdale and continued to be a famous English sportsman.

American 100-mile Record

1878 concluded with a spectacular 100-mile performance by **James Smith** at the Opera House in South Bend, Indiana. The track was extremely tiny, 30 laps per mile, 176 feet per lap, or 3,000 laps for 100 miles. It was a very dizzy 100-mile challenge, with 12,000 turns, that required a very attentive timekeeper. Smith fueled on 20 pounds of beefsteak and drank coffee and tea. "Up to the 50th mile (at 8:41:45), the pedestrian showed no signs of fatigue, but after he had passed that, his right ankle began to grow lame from the frequent turning of corners, and he slackened his speed somewhat. Many spectators came to watch, and in the evening, the house was full. Toward the end, the reaction of the crowd was intense. "

Smith reached 68 miles in 12 hours. "As the timekeeper announced the laps on the last mile, each one was received with applause, and the walker acknowledged it by a spurt which proved that he was not entirely exhausted. As the 30th lap of the 100th mile was announced, Smith was not content but spun around the track at a frightful speed and the audience could not cheer enough." He finished with a time of 18:26:30 and had broken the American best by 22 minutes.

CHAPTER THREE

Women Run 100 Miles

In 1878, women left their mark on the 100-mile sport in America, as the country became fascinated with their accomplishments. The most prolific 100-milers in 1878 were women. It was written, "One of the most peculiar features of the walking mania is the number of lady pedestrians now on stage, and the surprising speed and powers of endurance which they exhibit."

The 100-mile Women Pedestriennes

Following in the footsteps of **Madame Moore** of 1869, the first known woman to walk 100 miles in under 24 hours, more women started to compete in 100-milers in the late 1870s. Walking among women took hold in England. "The English girls are great walkers, and they diverge from the state roads and make excursions among the mountains." At the same time, there was concern about American women. "American girls are generally poor walkers, and it will soon be a difficulty to find an American lady who can walk more than twenty minutes without complaining of fatigue. They pay too much attention to the shape and make of their boots for pedestrian performances." But all that would change quickly as American women took center stage among American pedestrians during the late 1870s.

In 1879 it was written, "Although it has long been known as a singular fact that a girl who was too delicate to bring a pail of water from the well to the kitchen could dance half a dozen vigorous men, it was not until recent women made their wonderful walks, that the powers of lady walkists began to be appreciated."

Kate Wiltshire of New Zealand

Catherine Sarah "Kate" (Rider) Wiltshire (1853-1925) was an English woman who migrated to New Zealand when she was 19 years old in 1872. She met and married **Joseph Wiltshire** (1842-1906), a railroad man who had been an accomplished pedestrian in England. In 1873, in New Zealand, he accomplished the Barclay Match, 1,000 miles in 1,000 hours. Kate also took up the profession, achieving huge miles in exhibitions.

On May 5, 1876, **Kate Wiltshire**, age 23, only a few weeks after giving birth to a child, began her attempt to walk 100 miles in under 24 hours at the Auckland City Hall on a tiny track, about 28 laps to the mile. She walked in front of a large, enthusiastic audience, also entertained by the Milton Brass Band. Auckland believed that no woman had ever made this attempt in the entire world. She succeeded in walking 100 miles in 23:40. "The constant clapping of hands and waving of hats and handkerchiefs, as Mrs. Wilshire successively appeared at each corner, culminated at the last few rounds into a perfect furor of excitement." The band played "See the Conquering Hero Comes" as she finished, and the crowd hailed her (incorrectly) as the first woman in history to walk 100 miles in under 24 hours. Her husband, Joseph, would follow in her footsteps and walk 100 miles within 24 hours several times.

Bertha Von Hillern

MISS BERTHA VON HILLERN.

Bertha Von Hillern (1857-1939) was born August 4, 1857, in Freiberg, Germany. Her mother encouraged and trained her in activities of strength and endurance. She joined in with boys in walking contests and she would outlast them all. They would "gaze with mortified astonishment at the little figure, erect, quiet, moving silently and steadily on toward the goal."

She walked in several matches in Berlin and other European cities in her teens. In 1875, she emigrated to America at 18 to start a new life, even though she did not speak English well. She made her way to Illinois, continued walking and advocated athletic exercise for women.

In 1875, Von Hillern published a challenge in a Chicago newspaper: "I Bertha Von Hillern, herby announce my intention to exhibit my powers as a pedestrienne in a contest in this city, for the championship of the world, with any woman of unblemished character." Challengers came forward and, like the men, the women gravitated toward the six-day race where the bigger money existed.

Von Hillern was also a 100-mile walker. She trained hard for her first 100-miler, walking four hours per day and one hour of gymnasium exercise per day. She put on many 100-mile exhibitions, performing them between 27-28 hours. At Worcester, Massachusetts, it was remarked, "the now large crowd followed her very motion with eager eyes, the patter of ladies' hands and fans, and the waving of handkerchiefs preceding and following her like a wave around the hall." Von Hillern was the most prolific 100-miler among men or women during 1877-78, achieving that distance at least 12 times during a one-year period.

Von Hillern also made an impact on women's shoes, introducing "zero-drop" styles. A Kansas newspaper commented, "The female pedestrian of Washington, Bertha Von Hillern, walked 100 miles in 28 hours. She wears long, broad-soled shoes with low-heels, or without heels, and all the ladies of that wicked place are adopting her kind of shoe. Are there any "Berthas" in Kansas?"

Mary Marshall

Mary/May Marshall (1841-1911) started competing in 1875. Her real name was **Tryphena Curtis Lipsey**. She began competing when she and her husband were in serious financial trouble. She took up pedestrianism to raise sufficient money to pay a mortgage on a home in Illinois.

Marshall was 25 years old when **Daniel O'Leary** helped her train. After competing with Von Hillern in the 1875 six-day matches, Marshall also started to complete 100-mile walks.

Her first 100-mile event attempt was at the Music Hall in Boston, Massachusetts, during March 1877. "She started off with a fine burst of speed" at 8 p.m. Along the way, she experienced many issues, but preserved with "almost inflexible will power which called forth universal admiration." After 21 miles, she started taking frequent rests. At mile 83, her feet were so sore and swollen that she tossed away her shoes and walked the rest of the way in stockings. "The enthusiasm during her last mile was intense, the vast number of spectators present cheering her at the top of their voices and waving their hats and handkerchiefs as she put in two extra laps." Her 100-mile time was 26:47, much faster than Von Hillern's best.

Marshall tried again in July 1877 at New Bedford, Massachusetts, where she suffered terribly. "At times she would hold both hands above her head as if in extreme agony, and many ladies in the audience shed tears of pity. The committee begged her to stop, but when it was announced that she meant to continue, the large audience applauded enthusiastically, spurring on the fainting woman, who could hardly stand alone, and was almost carried around the track by men who held her up and hurried her on while they fanned her. The band played 'The Girl I Left Behind Me.'"

Marshall stopped competing in 1877 because she was with child. She returned for a brief time in July 1878 and continued for several years to perform various publicity stunts, including races against skaters and people pushing wheelbarrows.

Kate Lawrence

Kate Lawrence, age 30, was a dressmaker from San Francisco, California. She took up long-distance walking in 1877, believing that she could walk 100 miles faster than **Bertha Von Hillern**. She did serious training during 1877 to ease up her walking miles. Her first exhibition was at the San Francisco Horticulture Hall, where she reached 75 miles in 24 hours. "Mrs. Lawrence has walked daily to and from the city to the Cliff House, doing the sixteen miles in three hours for months before breakfast, and then doing her regular day's work."

Lawrence's first 100-mile attempt occurred in September 1877, in Pacific Hall in San Francisco. She finished in 27:40, about the same pace normally accomplished by Von Hillern. She repeated that journey in March 1878 at a pavilion in Sacramento, improving her time to 27:36:30. "It is the intention of Miss Lawrence to travel East and throw down the gauntlet, or rather the slipper, after demonstrating her pedestrian powers in San

Francisco." In July 1878, at Woodland, California, she finished 100 miles in 26 hours.

In August 1878, Lawrence was getting ready for her next 100-miler to be held in Virginia City, Nevada. A reporter was eating dinner in a restaurant when Lawrence came in. She asked for a private room and a square meal. He said she came in "with the frightened air of one avoiding the police." She

Pacific Hall (on second floor)

whispered her order to the waiter for a big thick steak, biscuits and coffee. "In a few minutes the order was filled, and the woman began to eat as if she had not tasted food for twenty-four hours. Between every mouthful,

Virginia City, Nevada

she cast furtive glances at the door, seemingly constantly expecting someone." Soon, a short man entered, searched the restaurant, and found Lawrence. He glared at her and took away her food. The man was her trainer, **Tom Kean**. She had been on a pre-race starvation diet prior to her 100-miler the next day. Kean was furious and screamed expletives. "Hell's Bells, this is the worst yet!" Then he took her by the arm and led her away, "like a husband who was conveying home an erring wife." After that exchange, evidently, Lawrence fired him.

The next day Lawrence walked her 100-miler at Virginia City. During that walk, her former agent tried to stop her walking by presenting a bond for an alleged debt. Spectators paid the bond, and the walk went on. "A large audience witnessed the close of the walk, and the excitement was intense."

M'lle Dupree

M'lle Dupree, (a.k.a. Madame Dupree) a French-American seamstress from Sparta, Wisconsin, started walking 100 miles in 1878. She was a mother and would at times walk miles with her eight-year-old daughter, **Minnie**. In May of that year, she made her 100-mile debut in Buffalo, New York, finishing in 26:45. But people were even

Stillwater, Minnesota

more impressed that Minnie walked five miles in 1:04:30. About a month later, Dupree improved her 100-mile time to 24:50 at Stillwater, Minnesota. She next set her goal to break 24-hours, a seemingly barrier for women.

But earlier, in 1877, **Carrie Parker**, a woman from Illinois, was said to have accomplished a 24-hour 100-miler. People believed it ruined her life and drove her to insanity. She was "a raving maniac," when she was brought before a court. "Her father testified that ever since the walking match, his daughter had been suffering with great nervous prostration and recently she suddenly conceived of the idea that her whole body was charged with electricity and she would not touch her feet to the floor." They sent her to an asylum.

Was a sub-24-hour 100-miler too tough on women? Dupree made her first attempt to walk 100 miles in under 24 hours in July 1878, at Association Hall in La Crosse, Wisconsin. They constructed a course laid with sawdust in the spacious hall, with 17 circuits per mile.

"At 9 o'clock p.m. Madame Dupree made her appearance dressed in white tights with a short over-dress reaching just below the loins, and a bodice without sleeves. She is a woman above the medium height, probably thirty-five years of age, well developed, but without superfluous flesh, and with sharp firm set, but not attractive face."

She walked with ease with full swinging steps and reached 25 miles in 5:42. During the night, some amateurs paced her, but her ten-minute-mile pace was too fast for them. She reached 50 miles in 11:49. "She was less flushed and there were signs of paleness. She changed her costume, appearing in a ballet dress." She reached 100 km in 18:50. In the end, she reached 91 miles in 24 hours and withdrew at the advice of a doctor. Her shoes seemed to be the biggest problem, leaving her feet swollen and blistered.

Dupree was still determined to try again and was finally successful at Mankato, Minnesota, with a time of 23:05 in September 1878. The next month in Cedar Rapids, Iowa, she walked 110 miles in 25 hours. During the walks, little Minnie would do impressions of **Daniel O'Leary**, delighting the crowds. Her

Mankato Opera House

son Frank walked one mile in six minutes. Indeed, she put on entertaining events, walking 100 miles about every month for a while. She was the fastest woman 100-miler up to that time and started to be referred to as "The wonder of the world."

In later years, Dupree engaged in fraudulent six-day exhibitions. Instead of competing against true women competitors, she would "compete" against relays of untrained men. Her tracks were never certified for distance and were significantly short of the advertised length. She claimed an unbelievable six-day world record of 492 miles against three men at an event in 1881 at Las Vegas, Nevada.

Exilda LaChapelle

Exilda LaChapelle (1859-1937) was a French-Canadian who began walking professionally in her early teens. When only 19 in 1878, she finished her first 100-miler during a 336-mile walk from Montreal to Toronto. Her 100-mile time was about 25 hours. She moved to Wisconsin, and repeated the accomplishment during April 1878, in Madison, Wisconsin, with a time of 25:52. People wanted her to compete against **Bertha Von Hillern**.

In May 1878, she again walked 100 miles, this time in Janesville, Wisconsin, with an outstanding time of 25:48. "The mayor, having heard that she had been compelled by her husband to walk against her will, tried to call her off the track, but she said, 'nobody could compel me to walk or to stop.' Plucky little woman!"

1878 was a banner year during the 100-mile craze, with well more than 100 finishes in America and England, including at least 22 100-mile finishes among the women. The six-day race emerged as the most popular race format for pedestrians that year, with about 15 races (men and women) involving at least 130 starters.

CHAPTER FOUR

100-mile World Records

By 1879, a remarkable shift took place. The most elite professional 100-mile walkers and runners became focused on competing in indoor six-day races for tremendous prizes and fame. That left room for amateurs to enter the sport and attempt to run or walk 100 miles for wagers or for nothing at all.

More of the general public started to hit the roads and tracks,

The Tramp Fever in the Hills.

trying to achieve ultra-distances on foot. The newspapers called this obsession "walking match fever," "tramp fever" or "pedestrian mania."

Pedestrian Fad

A Pennsylvania newspaper reported, "One of the most absurd manias that has recently afflicted humanity is the pedestrian craze which at present disturbs the mental balance of several cities in the interior of this state. The pedestrian craze infects lawyers, tradesmen and physicians. Half the population walk habitually on a dogtrot, and the police are instructed to see that amateur matches on the public streets do not interfere with the transaction of business. To what purpose is this waste of energy and enthusiasm?"

A Kansas newspaper wisely observed, "This is a great country for crazes. They sweep over the country like cyclones. Whence they come and whither they go, man knoweth not. Recently, the entire country was in the throes of the pedestrian craze. In every city, town and village athletes were wearily tramping around and around a sawdust circle, while thousands of spectators applauded the dreary exhibition. The men had had the red necktie craze and recovered from it in time to laugh at the suspender craze. America soon loves her fads to death."

It was wondered what craze would come next. "How would it do to inaugurate 'standing on your head' matches as the next? They would certainly draw, and the man who will first stand on his head for a thousand consecutive hours will go down to posterity and be remembered to the remotest generation."

Financial Impacts

For the successful ultrarunners of the time, the financial impact on their lives was significant. There has never been an era in ultrarunning when being a professional affected so many runners and brought in so much money. The amount that was successfully won in one race could be the equivalent of a lifetime's earnings. Managing that wealth was another challenge. **Edward Payson Weston** won an enormous amount of money during this era, but lived a lifestyle where he spent more than he brought in. He missed some key international events because he had to deal with legal troubles involving his finances. All this potential wealth also attracted greed and the potential for fraud.

1879: 100-mile Craze Continues

In 1879, many daring newcomers sought attention by trying the 100-mile distance either in races (matches) or in solo attempts. Newspapers reported more than 500 successful 100-mile finishes in 1879, including those in the more than 86 six-day races held worldwide. There were likely many more finishes that weren't reported. Newspapers announced many races to market the upcoming event, but often failed to publish the results. Professional women pedestrians continued to prolific in 100-mile events, with about 100 women finishes that year in 100-mile races and in the 18 women's six-day races.

The 100-mile craze occurred mostly in America but was also pursued at times in England and Australia. Those entering the sport included amateurs such as **Henry E. Nutting** (1856-1934), a member of Boston's YMCA gym, **Charley Joe**, a Native American from Michigan, postmen, mothers, and many young men in their early twenties.

100-milers in America

The Douglass Institute hosted a historic 100-mile race in Baltimore, Maryland, in March 1879. The Douglass Institute (named after **Fredrick Douglass**) hosted countless meetings of organizations promoting African American causes. This race was a unique contest for a couple of reasons. First, the course was on a very tiny track with <u>52 laps</u> to a mile on a hard floor with some sawdust sprinkled on it. That was only about 34 yards per lap! The two contestants were black, **Isaiah Hawkins**, age 41, and his nephew **James Williams**, age 19. Hawkins had no previous walking or running training. The race was planned to last 26 hours, and the prize was for $100. After 5.5 hours, the race was close with Williams at mile 21 and Hawkins at mile 20. After 26 hours, Williams was declared the winner with 89 miles. Hawkins reached 85. The attendance to witness the race was fair.

Mabel Scott vs. Ida Blackwell

In April 1879, two experienced 100-miler women, **Mabel Scott**, of London, England, and **Ida (Gifford) Blackwell** (1855-1936) of Boston, Massachusetts, faced off for a 100-mile match at the Music Hall in Boston.

"Miss Blackwell is a quick, nervous walker, while Miss Scott is most graceful and possessed of much staying power, so that a finely contested race will surely result." A month earlier, Blackwell walked 100 miles in 31:03:29 in Union Hall, at Cambridgeport, Massachusetts, and Scott walked 100 miles in 26:45:00 in St. James Riding Academy at Boston.

For this showdown, a large crowd gathered to witness the start, despite a terrible storm outside. The track was twenty laps to a mile. News coverage described the women more than the details of the race. "Miss Scott's hair was arranged in a twist with a single white rose on the left side."

Boston Music Hall

Blackwell took the early lead, but Scott caught up as Blackwell took rests. "A fine band of music was present and added to the enjoyment of the spectators as well as cheered the walkers." After 20 miles, Blackwell's ankle began to trouble her. Scott took the lead at mile 23 but accidentally hit her left ankle against an iron post, which caused it to swell up. Blackwell finally quit at mile 70 when she was 12 miles behind. The race was finally called at 27:54:09 when Scott had completed 89 miles. She quit once a 50-mile race between the two was arranged for the next month. Blackwell won that race by two miles.

Most women pedestrians turned their attention in 1879 to six-day races. At least 28 of these races were held for women, with about 150 starters. In these races, women did not reach 100 miles on the first day like the fastest men did. The best that year was probably the 92 miles reached by Amy Howard of New York City on the first day of the Women's International Six Day Tournament held in Madison Square Garden, where she broke the women's six-day world record with 392 miles.

Amy Howard

George Guyon

In April 1879, at Gilmore's Garden (Madison Square Garden), a 28-hour contest was held. **George W. Guyon** (1853-1933) reached 100 miles in 21:05:35. Guyon was a railroad man from Canada and Milwaukee, Wisconsin. Later in the race, a contender, Wall had serious trouble. "Wall, who said he was 21 but did not look to be over 18, fell apparently lifeless on the track while crawling over his 114th mile. His trainers placed him on some chairs and bathed and rubbed him with spirits for a few minutes when he showed signs of life. He was then placed on his feet, a white blanket thrown over his shoulders, and started on his journey again." He continued only for a few more laps.

George Hazael

What about speedy 100-milers? With "go as you please" rules, runners started to lower the best times. In 1879, the most elite ultrarunners of the time were taking part in several of the nearly 100 six-day races that year. Although they weren't competing in a 100-mile race, some races published split times, which are worth mentioning.

In April 1879, a six-day "Championship of England" was held at the Agricultural Hall in Islington, London, England. Contestants included famous Pedestrians, **Edward Payson Weston**, of America, **William "Corkey" Gentleman** (1833-), a vendor of cat food, from Bethnal Green, England, **Henry "Blower" Brown** (1843-1900), of Fulham, England, was a brickmaker who during his working days would run wheelbarrows up and down planks, and **George Hazael** (1845-1911) from London, England, the current 100-mile world record holder.

Hazael had been training hard for this race at the Sussex County Cricket Ground near Brighton, England. He was an experienced champion ten-mile walker and had been competing since at least 1870. He was also a true runner and ran the mile in 4:20:15.

Race Director **Sir John Dugdale Astley** (1828-1894) yelled "Go" at 1:02 a.m. All but Weston started to run fast. He went at his usual walking gait and took up the rear. Hazael built up a mile lead during the first hour. "Little happened worth recording in the early morning beyond the fact that Hazael continued to widen the gap between himself and the others, whilst Weston maintained his usual sure and steady mode of progression." Hazael reached 50 miles in an amazing time of 6:14:37 which was a world record for the 50-mile distance, about two minutes faster than the previous time.

By mid-day at mile 75, his potentially suicidal fast pace started to take its toll, and he had to lie down for 22 minutes because of stomach cramps. He was slower when he resumed, but quickly made up for the two miles that the others cut into his lead.

"Hazael still continued to widen the gap between himself and the others during the afternoon. A most unprecedented performance was recorded, namely the accomplishment of 100 miles by Hazael in 15:35:31, thus beating the fastest time for that distance by 1:28:35." In 1878, Hazael had set the previous record of 17:03:06, also at Agricultural Hall. Hazael finished second in the six-day race with 492 miles but had established himself as the world's best 100-mile runner. (Several years later, in 1882, Hazael became the first man ever to reach 600 miles in six days.)

Charles Rowell

Soon **Charles Rowell** (1852-1909) took over the crown as the fastest 100-mile runner of the 19th century, when he ran in the "International Pedestrian Six-Day Contest" held November 1880 in Agricultural Hall, in London.

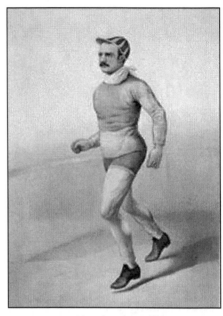

Charles Rowell

Rowell was born in Chesterton, Cambridge, England and was sometimes known as "the Cambridge Wonder." He had been hired as a pacer for Weston when he was barnstorming England, but later Rowell competed on his own. He soon won two world championship six-day races with at least 500 miles.

Unfortunately for this 1880 race, the weather in London had been very poor, preventing training outdoors leading up to the race. **George Littlewood** (1859-1912) of Attercliffe, Yorkshire, England was a speedy newcomer running in his first six-day event.

Agricultural Hall

The track was in good condition for the 1880 race at Agricultural Hall. It was seven laps to the mile, composed of "sifted garden mould, tanbark and a top dressing of sawdust." The race started at 1 a.m. Littlewood quickly settled into the lead but soon was passed by Rowell, who reached 50 miles in 7:38:44. The next closest competitor was about six minutes behind. At mile 70, Rowell led Littlewood by four miles. "At 13 hours Rowell began to put more distance between himself and Littlewood, who by that stage, had started to walk at times." Rowell reached

100 miles in a new world-best time of 13:57:13 in front of 2,000 spectators who cheered him enthusiastically. He smashed Hazael's previous record by about an hour and a half. Rowell went on to win the six-day with 566 miles, also a new world record.

Two others in this race also beat the previous 100-mile world-best, **John Dobler** (1859–1943), with 14:52:48, and **George Littlewood** with 15:19:30. **John Dobler** age was an Austrian-American from Chicago, Illinois. His 100-mile time crushed the American record by about 3.5 hours. His trainer was none other than the legend, **Daniel O'Leary.** A reporter at the race

Dobler leading Brown and Littlewood

commented, "Rowell's 100-mile performance is a most marvelous one, and far exceeds anything ever attained in long-distance pedestrianism, while Dobler's efforts are also far in excess of record."

100-mile World Record Broken Again

The 100-mile world-record would fall again in February 1882, to a mark that wouldn't be touched for another 55 years. A six-day race was put together to be held in Madison Square Garden in New York City billed as "The Race of the Champions." It turned out to be a very historic race. Leading

up to the race, **Charles Rowell** trained hard, sometimes reaching 40 miles in a day on the American Institute indoor track. "In the morning before breakfast, he will do about five miles, and then after breakfast, take a spin of twenty miles or so at the rink. Then a slight lunch, and a fifteen-mile run on the road would finish up the day."

Original Madison Square Garden

Rowell said, "I feel in first rate condition. I think I may give my competitors some trouble before they beat me." Asked about his race strategy, he replied, "I go according to what the other men are doing. My game is to beat the other men. I shall eat oatmeal, beef, tea, chicken, broth, eggs, chops, oysters, and nourishing food of that kind. My drink will be ginger-ale and sometimes bottled cider. I have no regular hours of eating but eat when I am hungry – that is pretty much all the time." When asked how far he planned to run the first day, he replied 150 miles. "My best first day's record is 146 miles in less than 24 hours."

The Madison Square Garden track was put into fine shape. Several strong truss bridges were constructed over the tracks to prevent the spectators from walking on it. Instead of a tanbark track, Rowell asked that it be made up of loam and sawdust which he thought would be much faster. The arena was heated by steam. "The excitement in this city over the six-day pedestrian contest at Madison Square Garden has almost reached a fever heat. The Garden was illuminated by 30 electric lights and decorated with flags and banners of all nations."

Right before the race, vendors were stationed at the Madison Avenue entrance trying to sell their race previews, shouting, "Lives of all the walkers" and "program of the race." An hour after the doors were open, 6,000 people were in the building with hundreds still waiting in line. The bookmakers with tin boxes sat at small tables operating near the scorers, taking bets. Rowell was a 2-to-1 favorite.

The race began on February 27, 1882, at 12:05 a.m. in front of 10,000 cheering spectators. They engaged **Patrick Gilmore's** 50-piece band to perform music during the race. After four hours, Rowell took the lead, followed closely by **George Hazael**. With the cramped track, some runners issued protests to the referee because of bumping taking place or they felt that their progress was being impeded by runners in the way. The referee took charge and made the participants stop complaining.

Rowell leading Littlewood

Newsboys woke up citizens at all hours of the night shouting the latest reports from the race. Bulletins were displayed on walls and dining windows in every block. A newspaper reported, "Tens of thousands of people, mostly fools, were eagerly asking, 'Who's ahead?'"

Rowell

Rowell reached 50 miles at the seven-hour mark with a ten-mile lead. He liked creating a good cushion to use in case he ran into trouble. It was rumored that massive bets were being placed on Rowell and that the bookies were not accepting any more money on him. "Rowell trotted along with his head bowed, and he evidently was figuring up his share in the profits. Although the crowd was large, there was less enthusiasm manifested than has been witnessed in previous contests. Excepting when the band of musicians gave vent to their feeling, the scene was almost funereal. The spectators stared at each other oftener than they did at the champions."

Rowell reached 90 miles in an impressive 12 hours. He went on to break his world record 100-mile time by

SCORE AT NOON.				
	Miles	Laps	Miles	Laps
Rowell	90	0	Noremac 75	1
Hazael	81	1	Sullivan......70	3
Hughes	78	3	Panchot......62	5
Fitzgerald	69	1	Scott 59	3
Hart	58	7		

30 minutes with an amazing time of 13:26:30. He reached 150 miles in just

22:30. The band played "Pinafore" and "He's an Englishman." Rowell did not make it to the end of the six-day race. He got sick and dropped out after about 415 miles. But **George Hazael** went on to win, with 600 miles, the first person to ever reach that milestone.

Amateur 100-Mile Record

Records were kept for amateurs separate from professionals. On August 26-27, 1881, **Archie W. Sinclair** (1840-1911) established the amateur 100-mile walking world record at Lillie Bridge, London, England with a time of 19:41:50.

On February 21, 1882, a 24-hour race was held in the American Institute Building in New York City for "The Amateur Championship

GO-AS-YOU-PLEASE.

Exciting Twenty-Four-Hour Race in New York Yesterday, in Which the Best Amateur Record Was Beaten.

of America" put on by the Williamsburg (Brooklyn) Athletic Club. There were 14 starters. Some walked and others ran. **James Saunders**, a Scottish-American living in New York, held the lead with 56 miles after nine hours. At about 13 hours, he passed 78 miles with a five-mile lead. He continued on and broke the known 100-mile amateur world record with a time of 17:36:14. He finally stopped at 120 miles, 275 yards in 22:49, also breaking the amateur 24-hour record by less than a mile. Despite being an amateur, it is believed Saunders received $100 for his win. Saunders would hold the amateur 100-mile record for about 20 years and the amateur 24-hour record for 26 years.

Geraldine Watson – World Record 100-miler

Geraldine Watson (1883-) was a schoolteacher from South Africa. She was a very tough individual who would set off on long walks up to 200 miles, carrying a small automatic pistol for protection. When she ran the Comrades Marathon (54 miles), unofficially in 1931, she received intense public attention. The first woman to run Comrades was **Frances Hayward** (1891-) who in 1923 finished with a time of 11:35. By 1931, the route was significantly faster with the road fully paved. Watson finished in a little over 11 hours, admitting afterward that she had nearly given up. She repeated in 1932 with a time of 11:56 and in 1933 ran an amazing 9:31:35, still unofficial because women were not allowed to compete. No other woman would run the race until 1965.

Watson entered a 100-mile road race organized in Durban, South Africa in 1934. The race was held on a circular road course. Watson ran a sub-24-hour 100-miler on June 30, 1934. She finished the race in 22:22:00, a fastest known world record time for a woman, despite strong gusty winds and rain. Two men also finished the race, **Fred Wallace** with a time of 16:52:20 and **Bill Cochrane** (1900-), with 17:25:00.

CHAPTER FIVE

100-mile Fraud

More of the general public started to hit the roads and tracks trying to achieve ultra-distances on foot. The newspapers called this obsession "walking match fever," "tramp fever," or "pedestrian mania." Ultrarunning historian **Andy Milroy** commented, "**Dan O'Leary's** 1877 and 1878 six-day wins in London created a huge stir in the US. It inspired ordinary people to undertake pedestrianism. Most could not afford the time to tackle a six-day, or even a 50-miler. That was beyond them. So, they became fixed on the 25-mile distance. There was an explosion of such events, newspapers wrote of a plague of such events gradually spreading out from New York." But the real money was in wagers to accomplish ultra-distances, 100 miles or six-day races.

Suspicious Races

As these 100-milers received intense public attention, widespread

The Pedestrian Fraud.

wagering took place. Skepticism arose whether these events and accomplishments were completely legitimate. In New York it was written, "People are beginning to awaken to the barefaced swindling which is being perpetrated in the matter of making matches. It may be doubted whether there has ever been a fair race since the day when O'Leary won the first Agricultural Hall race in London, in 1878. Matches upon which money is stacked and matches involving the suspicion of 'crookedness' are all the rage."

Purposeful Drugging

With high stakes wagering, greed motivated investors sometimes took things into their own hands. At Reading Pennsylvania, **Samuel F. Mishler** (1860-1931), a steelworker, from Reading, Pennsylvania was attempting 100 miles. After 15.5 hours at 70 miles, he asked for a drink of water. "Mr. Mishler says that a glass of water was handed him and that it had been drugged, for he was unable to continue to his walk. Others say he dropped to the floor in a swoon. He did not recover from the effects of the drug for several hours afterwards. When asked whether he thought he had been intentionally drugged, he answered 'Yes, because there was considerable money at stake.'"

Skipping Town

At North Adams, Massachusetts, alarming facts were revealed about a pedestrian, **William H. Dutcher**, (1848-), a railroad fireman from Poughkeepsie, New York. He had performed well in North Adams and won the citizens' admiration. Presents were showered upon him. He incurred debts around town based on his popularity and organized a grand ball where he would be featured. He sold many tickets but skipped town and didn't show up on the night of the event. It was soon also revealed that at his famed walking match, there had been cheating. His timers and judges had been bribed and credited him miles while he was actually sleeping.

Fixed Races

At the German Theatre in Davenport, Iowa, a 100-mile race was conducted and **Edward Miller** was declared the winner with a time of 23:22. His competitor, a **Mr. Collins**, had quit at

The Pedestrian Match a Fraud.

NEW YORK, March 2.—Whatever interest was felt in the walking match at the outset, is hourly decreasing. This morning the attendance was very slim. There is a growing feeling that the dropping out of leading contestants was due mainly to the fact that gate money and consequently the profits both to walkers and managers is likely to be small.

mile 88. Collins admitted he had purposely allowed Miller to lead him by several miles, that he had been bribed to do so in order that more bets would be made. "The agreement being made that Miller was to let him catch up and win the match at the close." People doubted his statement because Miller was the favorite anyway, but this illustrated that fixed 100-mile races likely did take place.

At Chicago, Illinois, an important "100-mile Championship of America" for $500 took place between professionals **William Edgar Harding** (1848-), editor of the *National Police Gazette* and **John Ennis** of Chicago. Harding had been sick for three days before the contest and continually left the track during the race. He quit after only 41 miles. Ennis covered the 100-mile distance and won. But it was reported in the betting circles that Harding had purposely sold out, a charge that one of Harding's backers emphatically denied. But with each race, there

JOHN ENNIS

were more and more skeptics about whether the sport was clean.

The prolific 100-miler **M'lee Dupree** didn't trust the timekeepers during her matches. She would mentally keep a record of every lap she completed and also what her competitors were doing. "In this way she was able to confirm the timekeepers' work whenever she chose and often did so."

At York, Pennsylvania, **Nelson** performed in a 100-mile match at the Laurel Engine House, trying to reach that mark in 30 hours. He was to push a wheelbarrow for the last 18 miles. He made it to mile 96 and suddenly quit, claiming that he could continue no longer. Fraud was suspected.

Frauds

J. H. Harriman, a 100-miler from Massachusetts, eventually used fraudulent

The New York Pedestrian Match a Fraud.

tactics. He once strode into Bismark, North Dakota, claiming that he had covered 100 miles in nineteen hours. But it was later revealed that his manager had helped him take a ride on a freight train to the city.

In 1885, **Professor Loring** advertised widely that he would walk 100 miles in 23 hours at Greenleaf, Kansas. A sizeable crowd showed up to watch, but Loring failed to appear. "It was noised around that Professor Loring was a big fraud. The management of the skating rink refunded the money to those who had gone to see him and at last accounts they were hunting for the aforesaid Loring with the City Marshall."

100-mile Interest Wanes

With each passing month in 1879, public interest was waning and crowds reduced. The six-day race had become far more popular for spectators because they were full of much more drama and suffering. One newspaper column commented on how the world had thought it was amazing when Weston had walked 100 miles ten years earlier in 1868. "But no one thought that in so short a time would his feat be considered a very ordinary affair. And now women have become imbued with the craze. Every female in the country has set to show what she can do. For no other reason than that of the notoriety gained. But it is time to drop it. Give us a rest! Why do not some of these persons who want to show their powers of endurance tackle a woodpile and see how many quarter cords they can saw in a certain number of quarter hours? There are a number of things they could do and should do."

At Rutland, Vermont, **Marie Vernon** began a walk at an Opera House but quit, "disgusted," because the audience was so small and she knew she would not make very much money. Her brother took her place to at least fill the obligation. It was reported, "Speculative walkists will no doubt give this place a wide berth in the future."

At Saint Paul, Minnesota, a highly publicized 100-mile race was a failure as one contestant just didn't show up. The other walker reached 100 miles in 23:45 but the event received little attention and a sparse audience.

Critics

As pedestrian events became more popular, increased voices from critics arose about the dangers and cruelty of the ultra-distance

PEDESTRIAN FRAUDS.

Blood Merchants of the Hippodrome and Their Victims.

sport, including 100-milers. Descriptions included audiences watching "the agonies of a half-dead man staggering along a track to the music of a band."

Watching two men who had walked 400 miles in a week was compared to seeing boxers who had pounded on each other's faces for three hours with their fists. "There is no grace, beauty or true manliness in them. The men who take part are on the intellectual, moral and physical level of prize-fighters, and it is hard to see wherein such matches are superior to the battles of the ring. In both, it is merely a question of the man who can stand the most suffering and still keep on his legs. What single good purpose was ever served by one of these degrading and brutal exhibitions?"

Violence and tragedies even occurred with the women pedestrians. At Westfield, Massachusetts 100-mile match, a competitor grabbed the hair of **Anna Berger** "and the struggle became one of hands instead of feet." At Milwaukee, Wisconsin, **May Fanning** fainted on the track and lay for two days in a stupor.

"As long a long-distance walker is tolerably fresh, there is little excitement in

—A pedestrian at Chicago walked one hundred miles for $100. He is a fool. He could ride twice as far on the cars for a hundred dollars. ◦

watching him. But once serious fatigue and pain set in, he does not see the crowd, which stares, and smokes. He does not hear the music, which mixes in a dream of the past life. He thinks that he is working in some country place that he knew long ago before he was a long-distance walker, and a mirage floats before him. Softer-hearted on-lookers wish to have some of the walkers removed, but their backer will not permit this."

"The New York 'blood merchant" hires some poor penniless lad who has the pedestrian fever and puts him on the track

A Pennsylvania man walked 100 miles to thrash an old school teacher for a licking received twenty-two years ago, but he returned a sadder and a wiser man. The teacher walloped him again.

and keeps him there until he drops from fatigue or exhaustion. The unhappy victim is forced into his tent and subjected to a course of treatment calculated to bring him to his senses or send him to his grave. Flogging the victim with wet towels and riding whips, running pins and needles into him, tweaking his nose, pulling his ears, kicking, thumping, cursing and swearing are among the many amiable attentions that the 'ped' is subjected to by his brutal attendants."

Why did these 100-mile runners and walkers do it? "Any reputation or popularity he may secure is extremely short-lived and is confined to the lowest classes. With few exceptions, they are handled by 'backers' who have them wholly in their power, who put up the stakes, pay the expenses, pocket the profits and too often sell out their men. The sooner we see the end of these races, the better."

People could even detect the impact that these grueling events had on their American hero, **Daniel O'Leary**. After some sickness when he still competed in a race. It was observed, "It was evident to every critical spectator that he had broken down and was fast weakening. He hardly walked a single yard without swerving from side to side, his steps describing a zigzag course. If you were to see him, you would be surprised. He is thin. His legs are not half so big as they were. He hadn't the flesh to carry him through, let alone the vital force."

During a six-day event in March 1879 at Gilmore's Garden, O'Leary quit after 215 miles. "He looked like a corpse. His face was terribly flushed, and his neck and chest were as red as a beet. He was the personification of a man who had walked himself to death." Rumors flew around that city that after he was taken to a hotel, he died. He did not. He recovered, but soon retired from competing in the sport.

100-miler Retirees

In May 1879, professional 100-miler **Edward E. Miller** could not find a challenger to race with him. He wrote in the newspaper, "I will now challenge the public at large to compete with me in the manufacture of a select article of either ice cream or lemonade. I agree never to be out of ice cream, which will be on sale every day of the week by the gallon, quart, or dish."

By 1880, many 100-milers evolved into novelty acts associated with fairs. The 100-mile attraction had worn off. There were much fewer 100-mile accomplishments mentioned in the newspapers.

By 1881, **John Ennis**, the well-known pedestrian from Chicago, also could not find challengers, so he turned to 100-mile ice skating. He defeated **Rudolph J. Goetz** (1851-) a champion long-distance skater from Milwaukee, Wisconsin. Ennis reached 100 miles on very rough ice, seven miles before Goetz, winning $100. His time for the 100-miles was 10:57.

100-mile 19th Century Craze Concludes

After 1882, 100-mile attempts, even by the amateurs, quickly disappeared, overshadowed by six-day races, and soon the accomplishments of those in

Hart	130.3	Dillon	104.2
Albert	130.1	Strockel	102.0
Guerrero	129.0	Conners	102.0
Golden	126.0	Sullivan	101.2
Panchot	125.1	Sinclair	100.2
Herty	122.0	Taylor	100.2
Day	118.1	Tilly	100.7
Hegelman	112.1	Vini	100.3
Cox	110.1	Stout	100.1
Moore	115.2	Noremac	100.3
Cartwright	105.4	Lurkey	100.0
Horan	105.2	Johnson	100.0

the 1870s were forgotten. But reaching 100 miles within the first day of a six-day race became common. On February 6, 1888, at Madison Square Garden, twenty-four men reached 100 miles in 24 hours.

By 1890 walks "around the world" took over the attention the fascination of Americans, especially as Jules Verne's Around the World in 80 Days novel became more widely read. Unfortunately, nearly all of these distance walkers fabricated their accomplishments once they discovered that the task was far beyond their abilities.

During the 1890s, 100-miler distance walkers returned to the outdoors, and at times, outrageous stories were printed in the newspapers. In July 1896, two men in Illinois walked 100 miles from Chicago to Rockford without stopping for food or rest. "Both are hypnotists, and they claimed that they hypnotized each other and imagined they were riding. This might be very useful to bicycle tourists whose wheels break down when they are at a distance from a repair shop or railroad station. But it is a little singular that two men should be able to hypnotize each other. How can that be possible?"

100 Miles Walking on Water

In 1896, **Robert Cook**, an inventor from Americus, Georgia, claimed that he walked 100 miles on Lake Ontario in 65 hours. People who had seen him perform said he was no fake. He invented water shoes that he claimed he could walk with as much ease and comfort on water as anybody could on pavement.

HE WALKS ON THE WATER.

"The shoes are a trifle over 4 feet long, 6 inches wide and 6 inches deep. The place for the foot is in the center and the shoe is strapped to it. The shoe is perfectly airtight. It is covered with white cedar wood, the bottom being of white hickory, which gives strength to the shoe. It looks like a small-sized canoe. A set of fins on either side of the bottom of the shoes operate in a peculiar way, securing a resistance to the water and preventing him from slipping backward or losing his balance." For months, he publicized that he would walk from Pittsburgh, Pennsylvania to Cincinnati, Ohio on the Ohio River, about 450 miles. It never happened. He was likely a fraud.

Edward Payson Weston's Christmas 100-miler

On Christmas Day 1896, **Edward Payson Weston,** age 57, tried to bring back some of his glory years' attention by attempting to walk 100 miles at the Ice-Skating Palace in New York City. A track was built on the skating floor, eight laps to a mile. They made the track four feet wide, out of boards with heavy paper covering them. At the start, Weston was introduced to the audience, who cheered him "to the echo." It was said, "His hair has turned white, but he looked remarkably well."

He started at 10 p.m. "As in former days, he walked with the same sprightly tread and carried a whip. As he made the first circle around the track, he was loudly applauded. He finished the first five miles in 58:20 and when this announcement was given out, he was again liberally applauded."

Skaters still went around on the ice as he walked on the outside. He told his doctor that his legs below his knees had gone to sleep, but this had happened before, and he wasn't concerned. "During the night Weston ran and walked alternately, and now and then reversed his way of going around the track. The coolness of the atmosphere in the Ice Palace did not appear to trouble him in the least."

In the morning, the skaters returned to the rink. "They livened the veteran pedestrian very much. Some of them would skate around the edge of the rink, keeping abreast of Weston, who chatted and joked with them." At 15 hours, he took his first rest. "During that time, he had eaten lots of eggs and calves' foot jelly and drunk beef tea, milk, and coffee. While he was off, he had a bath and changed his clothes."

After 19 hours, Weston's strength faltered, and a dizzy spell overpowered him. "He was assisted from the track as weak as a baby." His doctor worked on him and "soon the wonderful old man was up again and asking what it was all about." The doctor made him rest for nearly an hour. "He then appeared somewhat discouraged, but was cheered on by numerous friends. He soon struck his old-time gait and kept up bravely to the end." Weston succeeded and reached 100 miles in 23:56:30.

How many people finished 100-milers during the 1800s? It is estimated there were likely more than 1,500 finishes in less than 30 hours and several hundred were in less than 24 hours. Competitive 100-mile races took a hiatus at the turn of the century as attention turned to covering 100 miles on bikes, horses, or automobiles.

CHAPTER SIX

100-Milers Move Outdoors – Milwaukee to Chicago

From 1878 to 1908, six-day races were held indoors, where they were a unique spectator and gambling sport. In 1889, the home of pedestrianism in America, the original Madison Square Garden, was demolished. It had become a "patched-up, grimy, drafty, combustible old shell." A new, larger Madison Square Garden arena was constructed on the same site and opened its doors to a few more six-day foot races to the golden era of multi-day bicycle races.

Madison Square Garden II

1900 Bike race in Madison Square Garden

In the early 1900s, local laws in America were passed outlawing multi-day running and bike races. Indoor 100-milers ceased, and the 100-miler faced the threat of extinction again. In the former heart of 19th century ultrarunning, New York City, it was written, "These protracted tests of physical endurance serve no good purpose. They prove nothing beyond the fact that some men can force themselves to harmful exertion even when every fiber of their physical being is in active revolt."

But a flicker of life still remained in America. Starting in 1905, the 100-miler reemerged into the outdoors on the dirt roads in Illinois, thanks to some legendary marathon runners from Chicago who sought to attain the 100-mile distance. The route from Milwaukee, Wisconsin, to Chicago, Illinois, became the focus in America to test the 100-mile distance.

Albert Corey

Albert Louis Corey (1878-1926) was born in France. He served in the French army, where he became interested in athletics, especially in cross-country running. He competed in many races in his native France and gained a celebrated reputation. In 1900, he ran a marathon race in Paris. He also ran ultra-distances. During an 82-hour race, he reached an  astonishing 382 miles. He was also credited as holding the French speed record for running 40 miles.

Chicago Stockyards

Corey immigrated to America in 1902, went to work in the Chicago stockyards, and read that athletes were training at Marshall Field for the 1904 Olympic Games to be held in St. Louis, Missouri. He showed up one day in his running clothes, and after a quick running audition, was invited to become a member of the Chicago Athletic Association.

Even though Corey was not an American citizen, he competed at the 1904 Olympics in St Louis, Missouri, representing the United States. He ran the Olympic Marathon, which was on a tough course, 24.85 miles long and placed second with 3:34:16. He also won a silver medal in the four-mile relay race.

Thomas Hicks wins the 1904 Olympic Marathon

After the Olympics,

RUNNER TRAINS YEAR TO CLIP 100-MILE RECORD

Corey, of Chicago, Will Make an Attempt Next October to Set New Long-Distance Mark, After Competing in Two Marathon Races

Corey set his sights on breaking the 100-mile world record which he erroneously thought was established by himself of 16:22, while serving in the French Army. The world's best 100-mile time was 13:26:30, held by **Charles Rowell** of England. But perhaps Corey held the amateur record. **James Saunders** of England and Brooklyn, New York, was the recognized amateur 100-mile record holder with a time of 17:36:14, set on Feb 21-22, 1882, during a 24-hour race held in the American Institute Building in New York City. Corey's French run of 16:22 time beat that. At the age of 26, Corey said he had already run more than 30,000 miles.

As he trained, Corey had no set diet and lived on only two meals a day. He said, "I live mostly on meat and wine. I do not like to sleep very long. I am never in bed more than seven hours at the most, and I generally average about five and one-half or six hours' sleep a night. I get up every morning at 4:00 a.m. and run over to the Chicago stockyards where I work."

It was reported, "He weighs 139 pounds, five feet five, and has neither gained nor lost a pound in the last eight years. A hard day's workout, which means a run of from eight to fifteen miles, never fazes him in the least and he seldom loses more than a half-pound in weight. He is said to be one of the best proportioned and most ideally built athletes that ever ran on Marshall Field."

Milwaukee to Chicago: About 100 miles

Corey decided to go after a record running from Milwaukee, Wisconsin, to Chicago, Illinois, a distance of about 100 miles, depending on the route. **George Guyon** (1853-1933), a talented pedestrian and railroad man, was the first in 1876 to post a fast time between the two cities. He walked over the railroad ties, a distance of 85 miles in 23:25, with a moving time of 21:35. **Daniel O'Leary** was said to have accomplished the route in the 1880s, in 18:53. **Henry Schmehl** (1851-1932), a German-American and an early six-day pedestrian, completed the 100-miles in 19:54 on August 5, 1898, and earned the recognition as the record holder.

BETWEEN THE ACTS & BRAVO CIGARETTES

GUYON.
PEDESTRIAN.

COREY FELL FAR BEHIND THE RECORD

Corey made his attempt on December 8, 1905, crewed by an automobile. The rough dirt roads were more like a trail. It turned out to be in terrible condition, and he quickly knew that it would be very hard to break the record. "At places the roads were ankle deep in mud and Corey's shoes were coated with the sticky substance, making it really an effort for him to lift his feet. The automobile accompanying him ran out of gas and he attempted to go ahead alone. As a result, he lost his way and wandered about on the wrong route for three hours."

At Waukegan, Illinois, about mile 50, a large crowd came out to watch him run through town. He stopped for twenty minutes, was given a rubdown, and ate a light meal. His speed became slower and slower, and he eventually realized it would be impossible to

Waukegan, Illinois

break the record. He backed off his pace and just concentrated on finishing his long grind. At Fort Sheridan, the soldiers came out to give him a warm reception. **Corporal Sidler** tried to pace him for a while but gave up after a couple miles.

Chicago Athletic Association Building

He finished in front of the Chicago Athletic club with a large crowd waiting for his arrival. His 100-mile time was a disappointing 23:15 because it was truly a rugged trail run. He was wrapped in a blanket and hurried to a waiting carriage and was driven to his home.

Corey said, "It was simply impossible to make any fast time over the roads. At some places, it was impossible to run, and it was hard work to walk. I had a terrible time in the swamps north of Kenosha and wandered about for several hours trying to find my way. I was at last picked up by **William Hale Thompson** in his auto and found I was several miles out of my way. The heavy going tired me greatly and several times I was forced to stop to rest. Several miles out, I was paced by youngsters who came all the way to town with me. I think I shall make another attempt at breaking the record, as I am confident that I can do the distance in sixteen hours or less."

The First AAU Sanctioned 100-mile Race

In September 1906, a 100-mile race between **Corey** and **Alphonse "Alexander" Thibeau** (1885-1936), was arranged from Milwaukee to Chicago. It was put on by the Illinois Athletic Club of Chicago and sanctioned by the Amateur Athletic Association (AAU), the first 100-mile race ever sanctioned by the organization. **Alexander Thibeau**, a French Canadian, was another talented ultrarunner from Chicago who competed against Corey at the marathon distance. He was also an in-line ice-skating athlete.

Alexander Thibeau

The week before the race both of them did a multi-day trial run to find the best roads for the race to be held on. They accomplished about 25 miles per day in training.

The historic 100-mile race started at the Milwaukee Athletic Club headquarters at 9:00 p.m. in a drizzling rain on September 2, 1906. **Walter H. Liginger** (1861-1931), president of the Central AAU, shot a starting gun in the air, and they were off, followed by an automobile.

The race was a bust. Five miles out, the automobile's tire exploded, and the car had to be abandoned. The two runners did their best to plod along through ankle deep mud. Both dropped out after only 28 miles at the 4:20 mark, in Racine, Wisconsin. "The athletes floundered in mud on the main roads and were glad, doubtless, that the accident put an end to the long grind."

1907 Milwaukee to Chicago

Corey again made arrangements to go for the record, but on October 18, 1907, his attempt was postponed because of poor road conditions. "An automobile party reported the roads in such a condition that it would be foolhardy to attempt the long grind afoot."

Corey and Hatch

After a week's postponement, Corey made new plans. Another ultrarunner, **Sidney Hatch,** would pace him for the first ten miles. The plan was to run for 55 minutes during each hour and rest for five minutes.

On October 24, 1907, Corey started at Milwaukee at 9:00 p.m. in front of the Milwaukee Athletic Club. Four automobiles guided Corey and Hatch with headlights and a brilliant moon with perfect weather. Soon after starting, Corey was affected by stomach troubles, which greatly slowed him during the night. He stopped frequently and was rubbed down by his trainer, **Charles Wilson**. He ran sometimes five miles at a stretch without slowing to a walk, and other times would go only two or three miles between rests. At one point, both runners and automobiles lost their way, but soon got back on course.

Hatch bowed out at mile 35 and Corey continued. It was cold during the night. Corey's crew suffered, wearing heavy blankets in the cars, but they still didn't keep the cold out of the open-air automobiles. By morning, Corey had recovered.

"Corey ate little on the way. For breakfast, he had two eggs and a little milk. He felt for a time during the night as though he never wanted to eat again."

Along the way, they came suddenly upon a stream where there was no bridge. They lost time while his crew used some boards to construct a way for Corey to run across. His pace increased significantly and by late

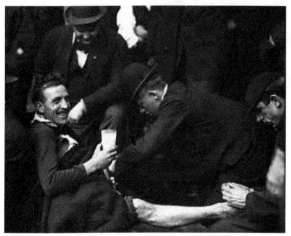

Corey with crew

morning, he was back an hour ahead of schedule. With a few miles to go, he ran strongly and was seen chatting with his crew as they drove along. "With the cheers of his companions and a large crowd of spectators ringing in his ears, Corey made a final sprint as he neared the First Regiment armory."

Corey finished in 18:33. It was written, "Corey's run was one of the greatest long-distance feats ever accomplished in this country." He lowered the fastest known time between the two cities by more than an hour. The former record holder, **Schmehl**, congratulated Corey at the finish.

ONE HUNDRED MILE RECORD SHATTERED BY ALBERT L. COREY

First Regiment's Great Long Distance Runner Covers Course from Milwaukee in Eighteen Hours and Thirty-Three Minutes.

RUNNER CUTS 81 MINUTES OFF 100-MILE RECORD

Corey was happy about the record but expressed disappointment that he did not run faster. He said he could have run much better if he had not been handicapped by illness and the condition of the roads. "I was feeling fresher at the finish than any time during the night and could have gone many miles farther with ease. I intend to try it again and will strive to make it in sixteen hours."

Sidney Hatch

SIDNEY H. HATCH

Sidney Herbert Hatch (1883-1966) was born in River Forest, Illinois. In 1899, he began his athletic career at Oak Park High School, running half-mile and mile runs. In 1904 he ran at the Olympic games in St. Louis in the marathon and finished eighth in a small field. He also competed on a 4-mile relay team the next day and won a silver medal.

In 1906, Hatch helped organize The West Chicago Harriers, promoting cross-country runs and trail races. Hatch developed his endurance as a newspaper circulation man, delivering papers on the run.

Corey, Thibeau, Armour and Hatch

That same year, Hatch broke into the news and received attention from the sport when he won the "All Western Marathon" (24.85 miles) with 2:47:24 on dirt roads in St. Louis, Missouri. He ran with fellow Chicagoan, **Alexander Thibeau** who finished in second. Hatch, Corey, and Thibeau dominated the marathons that emerged in the Midwest during that time, which evolved into a 1908-1910 "marathon mania."

In 1908, Hatch took part in a highly publicized 30-mile match race against his rival, Corey, to prove who was the greater ultrarunner. The race was held on a track at Harlem, Illinois.

Corey Quits Race and Hatch Stops at Twenty Miles

Corey injured his foot in the early stages and quit after only 17 miles. He had been in the lead. After 20 miles, finishing in 2:19, Hatch was declared the winner. Corey blamed his failure on a new pair of shoes. When he had taken off a shoe during the race, the nail on his big toe was out of place and his trainer made him stop.

In 1908, Hatch ran in the Olympic marathon in London and finished fourteenth.

1909 100-mile Race at Riverview Park, Chicago

Riverview Park

The "American Roller and Cycle Club" organized a 100-mile foot race in 1909 at Riverview Park in Chicago, Illinois, on a circular track. Seven runners were entered including Hatch who represented the Illinois Athletic Club. He had his eye on setting a 100-mile world record. At first, the course was going to be run on the boulevards of Chicago. Hatch wanted the course to run from Milwaukee to Chicago, but the costs would have been too great.

Sidney Hatch

A compromise was found to run the race on a turf course at the amusement park. Hatch had been successful a few months early on the same track when he won the "All Nations" Chicago Marathon.

For the 100-mile race, some elite runners were in the field. The starters included **Sidney Hatch, Charles Lobert, Olaf Lodal** (1885-1969), of Denmark, **Edward Von Kaenel, Erwin Arthur Theise** (1887-1984), **Hugo Fachs,** of Germany, and **Frank Frederick Mensing** (1884-1964), all living in the Chicago area. Lobert was the favorite. His claim that he was the best was the catalyst for organizing the race. He boasted he would break the 100-mile world record that they thought was held by Corey, of 16:33. Leading up to the race, the entrants trained together, taking long jaunts out in the country.

They held the race on July 24, 1909, and it started early in the morning at 1:32 a.m. Hatch held back, and others took the lead

Leader.	Distance.	Time.
Von Koenel [unattached]...	10 miles	1:15:07
Fachs [A. R. and C. C.]....	20 miles	2:45:24
Lodal [I. A. C.]............	30 miles	4:04:28
Hatch [I. A. C.]...........	40 miles	5:28:00
Hatch	50 miles	6:45:28
Hatch	60 miles	8:32:33
Hatch	70 miles	10:49:47
Hatch	80 miles	12:17:03
Hatch	90 miles	14:21:27
Hatch	100 miles	16:07:43

in the early stages. "Hatch showed wonderful judgment. He took the first quarter of his run in easy fashion, and never even tried for the lead." But by 31 miles, Hatch was in control and in first place.

Frank Mensing only finished 19 miles and quit after turning his ankle. **Von Kaenel**, who had led the race early on, dropped at mile 28. His shoes wore his feet raw. **Arthur Theise** stopped at mile 44 with stomach issues. After he took a rest and a short nap, he decided he was done.

Along the way, Hatch set a world's amateur best 50-mile mark of 6:45:28. At that point, he stopped for 15 minutes to be rubbed down. "Refreshments in the shape of three raw eggs and a cup of beef tea were given to him and he resumed the drill without any indication of fatigue." By

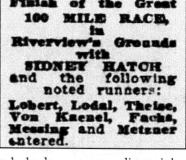

Finish of the Great 100 MILE RACE, in Riverview's Grounds with SIDNEY HATCH and the following noted runners: Lobert, Lodal, Theise, Von Kaenel, Fachs, Messing and Metzner entered.

mile 67, Hatch had a commanding eight-mile lead and pushed that to a ten-mile lead at mile 84 when he took a three-minute break to rub out some hip pain. It was observed, "Hatch seemed to be running more within himself than any of the others." During the entire race he was off his feet for only a total of 18 minutes. **Olaf Lodal** ran well until mile 71, when cramps seized up his left leg, causing him to quit.

Hatch won in 16:07:43, running the final mile in a blistering 5:19. "He made a good spurt at the finish and brought the crowd which had been watching the race to its feet, in a storm of applause." When he finished, Lobert was nine miles behind. While Hatch's 100-mile time was not an overall world record, it was a world amateur record and an American record. Only three finished, **Hatch, Charles Lobert** (17:33), and **Hugh Fachs** (18:00).

Hatch went on to dominate and win many marathons over the next few years.

1916 Milwaukee to Chicago

SIDNEY HATCH IS READY FOR 100-MILE RUN FROM MILWAUKEE TO CHICAGO

In October 1916, Hatch announced he would be going after another one of Corey's records, Milwaukee, to Chicago. While the course was likely considerably short of 100 miles, about 96 miles, it was still much longer than the 89 miles of Western States 100 in its early years. Corey's recognized record between the cities was 18:33. Competitors were solicited to make the event into a race. **Jesse Smith** was the event director. They planned to run the race through the night and finish at Grant's park, circling the track four times to add another mile, but they later changed the plan and added distance out on the road.

"Preparing for the run, Hatch took a twenty-hour snooze and a breakfast of soft-boiled eggs and tea. After a ten-mile walk, he went back to bed and slept until 6 p.m. A cup of tea and several slices of toast were all he ate just before the start."

Hatch, age 33, started at 8:00 p.m. from Milwaukee City Hall with a pacer, **Abraham Lincoln Monteverde** (1870-1964), a bookbinder from Johnstown, New York. Of Hatch it was reported, "He is in excellent training from running fifteen to twenty miles daily. To light his path during the night run, a searchlight mounted on an automobile was used." Officials of the AAU rode along to certify the run. They reported his run nationwide in newspapers. Hatch covered 7.2 miles during his first hour.

"Hatch wore long gray trousers, a jersey and mittens. Four automobiles convoyed the runner and for the first few miles out, a score of schoolboy athletes ran along with him. 2,000 persons gather to see Hatch and his partner off."

At Kenosha, mile 35, he stopped to change his shoes and had his feet rubbed. In ten minutes, he resumed his journey, making another stop at mile 50, at Waukegan, where he changed his shoes again. Monteverde dropped out at about that point behind about three miles.

"With a strong, cutting wind in his face, Hatch bent to his task and ran twenty-five miles more before he pulled up at Highland Park to drink hot lemonade and to have his legs rubbed." High school students turned out in Kenilworth to cheer him. "Hatch then ran all the way to the Rush Street bridge, piloted by motorcycles and mounted police, who stopped all traffic. When he reached the river, the bridge was raised, and Hatch lost fully two minutes." At that point, Hatch requested that the finish be at his Mystic Athletic clubhouse instead of at Grant Park. Work spread fast and a large crowd greeted him at the finish.

He stopped only three times (total time 20:30) for rubdowns and refused all food except orange juice and hot lemonade. His only stop during the night was at Waukegan, Illinois, at 4 a.m. when he received a rubdown. He ran the first 69 miles in 11 hours. Hatch's crew car, a six-passenger "Jeffery" did

HATCH'S RECORD RUN

Miles.	Time.	Miles.	Time.
5	39:32	55	8:37:35
10	1:24:17	60	9:24:52
15	2.09.45	65	10:09:25
20	3:00:00	70	11:01:25
25	3:50:00	75	11:45:02
30	4:35:03	80	12:37:47
35	5:19:40	85	13:20:26
40	6:10:00	90	14:03:03
45	6:55:47	95	14:45:32
50	7:41:02	95.7	14:50:30

not break down and proved that it could run at low gear on rough country roads. The company would use that in its advertisements.

Hatch finished the run on a "dog trot," and shattered the record, finishing in 14:50:30. After a brisk rubdown, he requests a bowl of ice cream. "After a short rest, he said he did not feel as weak as he had expected. He lost eleven pounds on the long run, his face was drawn, and his eyes sunken. His legs were sore, and he had blisters on the bottoms of his feet." He went to bed for a 24-hour sleep.

Officials of the AAU declared that Hatch's performance probably was the most remarkable in history. He broke what they thought to be the world 100-mile amateur record of 17:36:14 set by

> **SHATTERS RECORDS IN LONG-DISTANCE RUN.**
> Sidney Hatch, Makes 95-7 Miles In 14 Hours, 50 Minutes and 30 Seconds.

James Saunders in 1882. They correctly understood the professional world record was held by **Charles Rowell** with 13:26:30. Hatch's time was recognized as the American 100-mile record for decades.

Hatch Announces His Retirement

After racing in more than 45 marathons, winning about 20, and racing in more than 100 shorter distance races,

> **Sidney Hatch, of Chicago, After Long Career In Running Game, Will Retire**

Hatch, at the young age of 33, announced that he would be retiring from the sport. The 100-mile record was his ultimate quest, and he achieved it. With all his marathon finishes and wins, it was thought that up to that time, no man in history had ever competed in as many grueling races. Hatch was

called "the most famous marathon runner in the world" and it was said that he had won more marathons than anyone.

Before totally retiring, he announced he would run in the upcoming Yonkers Marathon and the 1917 Boston Marathon. But apparently Hatch had his eye on becoming a professional. It was rumored that he had entered a 72-hour race in Philadelphia. Once that went public, there was talk that he would be barred from running at Yonkers Marathon in New York. He insisted that he knew nothing about the race and claimed that the promoters falsely advertised that he entered the ultra-distance race. Hatch was allowed to run Yonkers and came in second place with 3:00:26. The 72-hour race in Philadelphia apparently was not held.

Hatch did not retire as announced. In February 1917 he finished fourth with 2:47 at the Pennant

> We got to hand Sidney Hatch credit for finishing fourth in the 25-mile Bronx marathon. That shows three guys were crazier than he was.

Marathon from the Bronx to New Rochelle, New York and back.

1917 100-mile Race for the Red Cross

Prior to running the 1917 Boston Marathon, Hatch announced he was interested in

SIDNEY HATCH'S AMBITION IS TO SET NEW 100-MILE RECORD

racing 100 miles again in an attempt to break 16 hours. "He keeps himself in shape by delivering newspapers around Chicago, running between 10 and 15 miles every day. Hatch is confident he can run 100 miles on a track in 16 hours. He is a clean-living man, has never smoked or drank in his life." The Morningside Athletic Club in Harlem was confident that they could get a race together with at least 10 entrants.

Hatch placed 2nd at the 1917 Boston marathon (25 miles) with a time of 2:30:19 and was referred to as "the runner of a hundred Marathons."

The 100-mile race was scheduled to be held May 25, 1917, but a week before the race, he notified the AAU that he had fallen and injured himself during a training run. Actually, he had broken a rib during a friendly boxing match and couldn't run for several weeks. It was decided to postpone the race until June 16th. The rescheduled race was promoted as a benefit for the Red Cross and was to be held in New York City. In early June it was written, "Hatch, who runs about as gracefully as a Jersey cow being chased by a milkmaid, is grinding out from 15 to 20 miles a day in preparation for the race."

The race was never held for some reason. In April 1917, the United States broke away from neutrality and joined in World War I, by declaring war on Germany. In

June 1917, American combat forces were being shipped off to France. The focus on the war likely canceled the race.

In October 1917, it was announced that Hatch had enlisted in the infantry and was anxious to get over to Europe to fight in the war. He turned over his newspaper circulation business to a friend. "Hatch should be a star in track for many years to come and the company  that lands his services will no doubt be proud. Hundred mile runners are scarce and men like Hatch will play a big part in this great war." He immediately participated in military relay races held in the States.

The Great War Halts American 100-milers

As World War I raged, 100-milers and ultrarunning in general was sidelined for a number of years. Even the 1918 Boston Marathon was canceled, and a military relay race was held instead. In 1919, the Logan Square Athletic Club of  Chicago announced they would be holding a Milwaukee-Chicago 100-mile race two-man relay race and advertised that Hatch would likely participate. The race never took place.

Where Did They Go?

What happened to the great ultrarunners from Chicago?

Sidney Hatch

Sidney Hatch ran in races during 1918 for the army, promoting the war effort for Liberty Loans. Later that year, he went to France. He was first attached to regimental headquarters as a runner, but he asked to be transferred to the front lines on a cannon gun crew. He hauled guns and was the battalion runner, taking messages to and from headquarters.

During an October 1918 battle near Brieulles, France, as Hatch was taking a message, shells began to fall. He dodged into a hole and was buried by a blast. After being helped out, with his leg wounded by shrapnel, he continued to take the message to headquarters. "It was a thousand yards down 'the death path' and the ground was popping with shells. It was a real death patch, but Hatch swung down it with the same ease he might start a championship marathon race." He made it and ran back with a message response.

Hatch was decorated for "extraordinary heroism" and was awarded the Purple Heart and Distinguished Service Cross. He returned home to Illinois as a hero in May 1919.

After the war, he ran in two more Boston Marathons before retiring from competitive running. He became a postman in his hometown of River Forest, Illinois. He married, had three children, and retired from the postal service at the age of 70.

Sidney Herbert Hatch, the greatest American 100-mile runner of his era, died on October 17, 1966, exactly 50 years to the day after he made his famous 100-mile run on October 17-18, 1916. He was 83 years old. There was no mention of his running accomplishments in his obituary.

A modern-day Milwaukee-Chicago 100-mile Turkey Trot is held yearly to raise money for ALS research.

Alexander Thibeau

Alexander Thibeau was selected by the United States to run the Olympic Marathon at the 1908 London games but did not start. He was a machinist by trade and broke the world's amateur indoor marathon record in 1909 with a time of 2:52:51. But soon he turned professional in May 1909, in order to enter a $10,000 international 26.2-mile marathon race held that started at White Sox Park. Thibeau finished the race in last place among the eight starters. His career faded significantly. In 1911, he took part in a six-day relay race (five hours per day) put on by **Daniel O'Leary** at Tomlinson Hall in Indianapolis. At the age of 42 in 1927, he placed second in a marathon with a time of 3:10. He died in 1936.

"Besides having scores of victories to his credit as a runner, he has attracted considerable attention as a wrestler, skater, boxer, and walker. He is the possessor of a large collection of trophies, including solid gold medals, some of them diamond studded."

Albert Corey

Albert Corey finished 4th in the 1908 St. Louis marathon. Club members, Hatch and Thibeau, finished ahead of him. That year, France sought to have Albert Corey represent his homeland in the Olympic Games. He passed on that, wanting to run again for America. But it was too late to add him to the US team. "Corey was indignant at being left off the team and charges the failure to name him to 'spite-work.' He has practically given up the hope of taking part in the marathon at London and is now only sorry that he didn't take up the offer of French authorities."

NOT IN HIS CLASS

Albert L. Corey No Match for Dorando M. Pietri in Marathon Race at Chicago.

FORMER CLAIMS INJURY

Virtually Quits After Two Miles and Italian Finishes Miles Ahead of Him.

Corey was called "Champagne Charley" by his competitors because of his free use of the wine during races as a stimulant. He used it openly during his Chicago Marathon win in 1908.

In January 1909 Corey ran a match marathon in Chicago against Italian great, **Dorando Pietri** (1885-1942) who had finished the 1908 London Olympic Marathon in first place, but later was disqualified because of help received when he kept collapsing with a few yards to go. The match race was a bust when Corey started limping after only two miles because of a sore ankle. "Corey gave a miserable account of himself, whether by accident or just because he knew he was up against a better man." Pietri won alone in 2:55. Doctors could find nothing wrong with Corey's ankle. He was branded a coward by the press and his running career was over. He died at the age of 48, in 1926.

CHAPTER SEVEN

London to Brighton and Back

During the early 1900s, a remarkable shift occurred. In the late 1800s, America was the home for ultra-distance walking competitions. But as pedestrian competitions fell out of favor and outlawed in the US, ultrawalking ceased for a time. The shift went back to the old country and 100-mile amateur walking competitions eventually became very popular in England.

London to Brighton

More than 100 years ago, there were a few venues and courses that had a significant impact on the history of ultrarunning, 100-mile races, and endurance sports in general. These include Madison Square Garden in New York City, Agricultural Hall in London, and above them all, the **London to Brighton** route (52+ miles) in England.

For many decades, whether on foot, on bike, on horse, or in an automobile, the road to Brighton was the place to race, including 100 miles on foot. Eventually many ultrarunning legends would compete on the Brighton Road including **Don Ritchie, Cavin Woodward, Ted Corbitt, Eleanor Robinson, Sandra Kiddy, Donna Hudson, Alastair Wood, Bruce Fordyce, Park Barner, Stu Mittleman, Jim King, Ruth Anderson**, and **Frank Bozanich**. London to Brighton was traditionally a one-way race of 52-55 miles,

Brighton

but in the first half of the 20th century, it was also used to compete 100 miles by walking or running a double London to Brighton.

In the mid-1800s, the seafront affluent resort city of Brighton became very popular, as the railroad was built from London, about 52 miles away. Prior to that, people came by horse coaches that made the trip multiple times per day with ever-increasing speed.

Brighton was a city of the upper class and featured an aquarium, which opened in 1872. It included marine exhibits, a 100,000-gallon tank, sea lions, an octopus, and a distinctive clock tower and gateway. It was also the site for organ recitals, concerts, lectures, and exhibitions. Day trips to Brighton became popular and railroad speed records were set for the route.

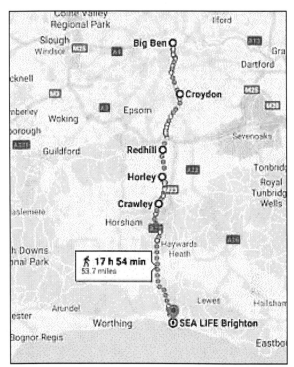

The road to Brighton was measured from the Big Ben clock tower north of Westminister Bridge in London to the Aquarium in Brighton. The clock tower was completed in 1859 and at the time was the largest and most accurate four-facing striking and chiming clock in the world. The tower stands 315 feet and is found on the north end of the Palace of Westminster. London to Brighton ran across River Thames on Westminster Bridge, which was originally completed in 1750, and replaced in 1862, the oldest bridge still crossing the Thames.

The original course went through the towns of Croydon, Redhill, Horley, Crawley, and Cuckfield. Over the years, the route competed increased in distance somewhat with the creation of modern roads and more towns to go through.

Early Cycling London to Brighton

Participants in the new sport of cycling started to ride along the route. This would soon prompt runners and walkers to try it as well.

As early as 1869. **John Mayall Jr.** (1813-1901) was the first person to reach Brighton from London by velocipede. He accomplished it in 12 hours, in time for dinner, and then he attended the second half of a concert in the Grand Hall. Soon afterwards, **C. A.**

John Mayall

Booth pressed harder to better the fastest known time to 9:30.

In 1870, **T. Moon**, "an expert bicyclist" set the first fastest known road cycling time on the route of 5:40. A few days later, he accomplished a double Brighton Road, 104 miles in 15 hours. He stopped for breakfast, a lengthy lunch, and took a break for tea along the way. A couple of years later, the Amateur Bicycle Club promoted a cycling race to Brighton, which was won in 5 hours, 25 minutes.

Early London to Brighton on Foot

Traveling on Brighton Road on foot obviously occurred for centuries. In July 1803, **Captain Robertson** walked from Brighton to London and back in 45 hours, more than 100 miles, and repeated the feat in November of that year, covering the first 53 miles from Brighton to Westminster Bridge in 14 hours. In December 1825, a

Mr. Tomlinson ran 9:50 from Brighton to London.

Racing on foot from London to Brighton started early, even before cycling races. The first known running race was conducted on January 30th, 1837, when two professional runners, **John Townsend** and **Jack Berry** competed. Townsend, 45, known as the "Veteran" won in 8:37. Berry quit with four miles to go.

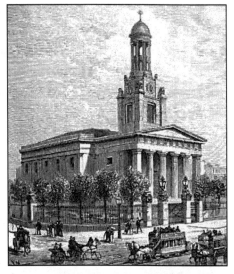

Years passed, but more attention was given to pedestrian feats on the road when **Benjamin Trench** of Oxford University accomplished a sub-24-hour 100+-miler in 1868 by accomplishing a double. He walked from Kennington St. Mark's Church to Brighton and back in 23 hours for a heavy wager.

In 1869, **W. M. Chinnery** and **H. J. Chinnery**, two well-known amateur runners, members of the London Athletic Club, walked London to Brighton in 11:25. It was written, "This feat is almost unparalleled in the recorded feats of modern amateur pedestrianism."

St. Mark's Church in Kennington

By 1876, wagers began to influence accomplishments by foot on the famed road. **Sir John Lynton** was offered 1,000 guineas on a challenge to wheel a barrow from London to Brighton in 15 hours. He accomplished the bumpy trip easily, wheeled a bamboo barrow with handles six feet long, and dressed in a "running costume."

In 1878, **P. J. Burt** claimed the official fastest known time on foot with 10:52, using a starting point at the clock tower on the north side of Westminster Bridge (Big Ben) in London to the Aquarium in Brighton which turned into the standard start and stop point.

More matches took place. In 1885, **C. L. O'Malley**, an accomplished athlete, walked against a competitor and lowered the record by more than an hour. A barefoot competition was conducted on the Brighton Road in 1882. The furthest competitor with bloodied feet, almost made it, but fainted in pain with four miles to go.

By 1897, large foot races were held from London to Brighton organized by the Polytechnic Harriers. That year there were 37 starters. The winner, **Edward "Teddy" Knott,** (later the founder of the Surrey Walking Club) finished in 8:56:44. At that time, he was credited as the first to cover the distance on foot in less than nine hours. "Go as you please" walking or

Polytechnic Harriers

running races began on the course in 1899 with 14 starters at Big Ben. The winning time was 6:58:18. In 1902, cyclists showed off, and demonstrated that they could ride the course to Brighton and back, 104 miles, in a shorter time than runners could do one trip. They succeeded in 5:50.

Horses and Automobiles

Even horses got into the game in 1888 when "Ginger" was driven at a trot to Brighton in 4:16:30. They increased the speed limit on the road to 14 mph, allowing automobiles to compete along the route in 1896. The race was called "The Emancipation Run" to celebrate the passing into

law of the "Locomotives and Highways Act" of 1895, which removed slow speed limits and abolished the requirement for these vehicles to be preceded by a man on foot waving a flag. That year, 33 motorists started from London and 17 arrived at Brighton. About 10,000 cyclists also joined in.

1902 London to Brighton and Back - 104 miles

Edward "Teddy" Knott (1859-1929) of Kensington, established The Surrey Walking Club in 1899. He was known as "the father of road walking." Knott was an exceptional athlete excelling in boxing, swimming, running, and cycling. The club was the first athletic club in the United Kingdom that specialized in walking and sped up the popularity of the sport. Members took part in racewalking events and country strolls. Their club headquarters was at the "Swan and Sugar Loaf" in South Croydon, south of London, a popular refreshment stop on Brighton Road. The landlord, **John Brown,** was a generous supporter and host of the club.

The Surrey Walking Club stepped into 100-miler history on October 31, 1902, when they held the first "London to Brighton and Back" walking competition, with a distance of about 104 miles. Instead of using the traditional starting point at Big Ben, the race started and ended

Club headquarters in South Croydon

at the club headquarters, about ten miles to the south, in South Croydon. With the new starting point, the route still covered the entire London to Brighton course twice, for 104 miles.

A crowd of several thousand people turned out to see the historic start. It was reported, "One of the most important affairs in road walking contests was the London to Brighton and back race of the Surrey Walking Club. Ten hardy 'walkists' turned out. The start took place at South Croydon, from whence the walkers had to pass by Westminster clock tower, thence to Brighton Aquarium and back the same route." **Jack Butler** won, with an impressive time of 21:36:27. Two others finished in less than 24 hours, **G. H. Schofield** and **W. J. Taylor.**

The walkers in England set a new 100-mile standard and wanted to demonstrate their abilities by reaching 100 miles, going from London to Brighton and back. A couple weeks after the

The newspaper had the wrong mileage

initial race, **L. Novelli,** a hotel owner at Brighton, wanted to prove that he could accomplish it in less than 24 hours. "Accompanied by an automobile and a couple of friends, the walkist started off at a brisk pace. Nothing of note happened until the pedestrian ran into a dense fog and the chauffeur had to go on in front and climb the finger posts to find out the way. This state of affairs continued for three miles, when on trying to jump out of the way of a passing auto, Novelli slipped on the roadside and fell." He sprained his ankle but tried to walk it off. The fog grew worse, forcing him to stop for a while. He eventually made it to Brighton, four minutes over, in 24:04. The story about his attempt was published as far away as Canada and the United States.

1903 Stock Exchange London to Brighton

A historic race took place in May 1903, that truly brought "London to Brighton" into the public spotlight. Early in 1903, **William Bramson**, a member of the London Stock Exchange, tried his own walk from London to Brighton. He accomplished it in 12:30. This sparked the idea of organizing a company-wide walk.

The Stock Exchange had been suffering through a slow economic time with poor morale. Company executives decided a walk would help the situation. Entry into the 52-mile race was free, but they could win monetary awards. The press gave the event intense attention. Entrants started furiously training. Some people even employed professional trainers.

Members were seen striding through the countryside roads on the weekends. Large wagers were made on race results.

One reporter wrote, "Their refreshments, I am told, will consist chiefly of beef-tea and the like, stimulants only being employed to restore suspended animation. I am also given to understand that all the starters were to be sent off in one batch, presumably with their attendants mounted on bicycles in following at the distance of one yard."

The Start

The race was held on May 1, 1903, (May Day, a bank holiday) with eighty-seven starters, who began from Big Ben at 6:34 a.m. Most of them were young stockbroker's clerks.

"Half of London seemed to be abroad on foot or awheel to be present at the start. At a very low estimate, there must have been 30,000 people in the immediate neighbourhood of Westminster, the bridge itself being covered with them as closely packed as they could stand. The 87 competitors went first, headed and surrounded by very necessary mounted police, who had a hard struggle to protect them from the admiring throng. The nine official cars followed in a long string, then the unattached motorists and, last of all, a confused mob of bicycles and pedestrians struggling forward in the rear."

Advertisers took advantage of the situation and motored through the crowd with signs such as, "Why walk, when you can buy a bicycle for next to nothing?" Many refreshment vans also went through the crowd. The weather was pleasant, but the road was muddy from a deluge the night before.

"Crowds stood four to five deep upon the pavement the whole way to Kennington. At first the walkers kept fairly close together, with the exception of some few unfortunates who got swallowed up in the following throng."

The Finish

All crossroads were alive with people all along the route. It seemed like a public festival was being held. Flags were put up across the road. "The remaining seven miles to the winning post became more and more of a popular ovation. Horsemen, motors, and innumerable cyclists poured out of Brighton in a continual stream to meet the on-comers."

The finish line was near the entrance to the Brighton Aquarium, and the square was overflowing with people. A large police force tried to manage the crowd. A smart advertiser caused a false alarm as an imposter dressed in running clothes came

2. G. D. Nicholas	9	33	53
3. T. E. Hammond	9	35	7
4. R. Davis	9	35	21
5. W. L. Nicholas	9	40	40
6. N. Varley	9	41	50
7. J. H. Murray	9	49	9
8. H. A. Dunkelsbuhler	9	56	13
9. H. N. Duke	9	56	27
10. John H. Childs	9	59	28
11. George Hoare	10	3	48
12. F. East	10	4	2
13. J. T. Jull	10	6	21
14. S. E. Knights	10	9	31

down the road with a placard pasted on his back, telling the crowd where to dine.

The true winner, **E. F. Broad**, struggled through the mob of admirers and reached the winning post in

9:30:01. Seventy-three finished within the 13-hour limit for the 52 miles. "Some of the men, especially among the later arrivals, were terribly exhausted by their long task. One or two of them absolutely collapsed and had to be carried from the ground."

This event truly started a walking craze on the road to Brighton and was a historic milestone event for the future of ultrarunning.

1903 London to Brighton and Back

On November 6, 1903, they again held the double Brighton, establishing a long 100-mile British tradition for

decades. America noticed. "Road walking still continues to hold popular attention in and around London. Events given by the Surrey Walking Club are always productive of something rare, but this one recently from London to Brighton and back revealed the most astounding bit of road tramping ever seen in England and incidentally lowered the record by a big margin."

The 1903 start was again at South Croydon. The walkers started at 9:22 p.m. The leader, **F. J. Wakefield**, covered the course's out-and-back to London's Big Ben (21 miles) in 3:52. The walkers encountered thick fog at Southam Bottom. But after a little tea at the Temperance Hotel, they forged ahead.

In the morning, a large crowd was gathered at the turnaround point at the Brighton Aquarium. **Harry W. Horton**, a member of the Herne Hill Harriers, arrived first, followed 15 minutes later by **Wakefield**. The leader's time for the 100 km distance was 12:08. Horton, seeing how far he was in the lead, pushed on hard, reaching 76 miles in 14:50, and 94 miles in 18:23, well ahead of **Jack Butler's** course record. With just a mile to go, Horton was struggling, but a glass of champagne revived him. He finished the 104 miles in 20:31:53. Five walkers beat 24 hours.

Cyclist vs. Walker

A friendly rivalry existed on the Brighton Road between cyclists and walkers. In 1903, a "curious match" was put together on the road between a **Mr. Bellingham**, a walker, and a **Mr. Young**, a cyclist. Bellingham was to walk 41 miles from Croydon to Brighton while Young had to cycle from Brighton to London and back, 104 miles. Huge wagers were bet on the race. Friends crewed both competitors in automobiles.

Both started at the same time at 4:30 a.m. The two met near Horley, mile 15 for Bellingham, and 28 for Young. They shouted friendly

HUMBER CYCLES
STILL LEAD IN DESIGN.

The New Humber Rim Brakes were the Greatest Novelties Exhibited on Cycles at the Stanley Show.

Prices, £10 10s. to £22 10s.

HUMBER, LIMITED, 32, HOLBORN VIADUCT, LONDON, E.C.

encouragement to each other. Young reached Big Ben, his halfway point, in 3:35. He had fallen, hurt his arm, and had two flat tires along the way. He also had to battle automobile traffic. With five miles to go, Young on his bike overtook Bellingham, finishing his double Brighton in 6:48.

Bellingham finished his 41 miles in 7:48. "The cyclist had thus traveled at a rate of over fifteen miles an hour and the walker at the good rate of over five miles an hour. It was a capital race and showed that people had accurate notions of the relative speeds of cycling and walking."

Horley. Brighton Road.

Thomas Hammond

Thomas "Tommy" Edgar Hammond (1878-1945), was a London stockbroker. He was a tall lanky walker, more than six feet tall. Hammond broke into prominence in the sport when he placed 3rd at the inaugural Stock Exchange London to Brighton walk held in 1903. He continued to improve, and the following year won the London to Brighton 52-mile version with a record time of 8:26:57. Hammond joined the Surrey Walking Club and became very involved in the sport. In 1907, he progressed to being recognized as a "world's best" ultra-distance walker when he won London to Oxford (55 miles) in 8:51:14. His walking style was described as "a striking combination of ease and efficiency one could hardly imagine."

The 1907 Brighton and Back 100-miler

After a four-year absence, they held again London to Brighton and Back on June 21, 1907, with six competitors. Only members of the Surrey Walking Club were eligible for the race. Those who finished in under 22 hours would be awarded a gold medal, a gold center for those 22-24 hours, and a silver medal for those 24-26 hours.

Hammond was the obvious favorite going into the race. Despite not being invited, a member of the Manchester Athletic Club, **A. R. Edwards**, ran the race "bandit" with his own staff of timers and "two automobiles full of edibles of all descriptions, including beef, chicken, eggs and jellies and liquor from champagne down to aerated waters and there was a spirit lamp too, to boil the kettle if it was wanted." The other runners only had a solitary cyclist carrying refreshments for support.

Tommy Hammond

Croydon Tram

The start was again at the "Swan and Sugar Loaf" in South Croydon. In the evening, at 9:04 p.m., after the word "Go" was yelled, Edwards jumped into the lead, going at a great pace. "The course for nearly three miles was by tram lines, and the cars, automobiles, and spectators who ran in front made the going difficult for the walkers." Edwards was pressed hard by **Bill Brown**. After a mile Edward's crew pleaded with him to back off, that the race was for 100 miles, not one mile. But he ignored them and kept "pegging away." Brown and Edwards traded the lead for the first few miles.

"Nearing Westminster Bridge, the traffic was much congested, and when Big Ben came in sight, Brown's lead had reduced considerably. The clock tower marked 10.5 miles of the journey." Brown reached there at 1:35:24, Edwards at 1:23:55, and **Tommy Hammond** at 1:38:07. "As they reached the Canterbury Music Hall, Edwards dashed ahead and quickly took a big lead and seemed to draw away from his opponents in every

Canterbury Music Hall

Surrey walking team, middle, Tommy Hammond with Bill Brown to the right

stride."

At the 21-mile point, Hammond finally took the lead and never looked back. Edwards did not worry and said, "He'll have his bad time shortly. He's a long way from home. Lamps were lighted as a few spots of rain came down. The moon was covered with a mist, and it looked as if the walkers were in for a drenching, but in a short time the weather cleared." Others caught up to Edwards. After pushing forward in great pain, he finally quit after being on the road for eight hours.

"The roads, although rough in places, were on the whole good, and a stiffish breeze tempered the rays of sun." Hammond held to lead at 50 miles, reaching that point in 8:26. "Hammond put in some fine walking at this point, and although a strong wind blew against him, his time was truly remarkable. Keeping up the pace, he swung around the official timekeeper at Brighton Aquarium (100 km) in 10:30:36." He had a 90-minute lead on the others at the turnaround.

Tommy Hammond

"Hammond started on the homeward tack. The going was frightful on account of the dust kicked up by automobiles and cyclists. At every mile Hammond increased his lead and with victory in sight, he again reeled off more than five and a half miles to the hour. Hammond passed the winning post wonderfully fresh and well. He got a great ovation from the crowd present."

Hammond in horse trough

Hammond finished the 100+ miles in 18:13:37, crushing the fastest known time. He reached the 100-mile mark at 17:25. It was called, "The most remarkable walking feat of this or any other generation."

105

"The secrets of Hammond's success are his perfectly natural style of walking. A pace of six miles an hour is to him, apparently an ordinarily easy rate of progression. Standing 5 ft. 11 inches high and of comparatively slender build, Hammond gets a long stride without seeming to do in owing to his rapid leg movement. His age is still well on the right side of thirty, so further honours in the record-breaking way doubtless await him."

1908 Middlesex Walking Club 24-hour race

On September 11, 1908, the Middlesex Walking Club's 24-hour track walking race was held with 39 walkers at the White City Stadium in London, England. Judges were in place to make sure walking was enforced. It was thought to be the first 24-hour track race in 20th century England. (There were others held earlier in America). Hammond again was the clear favorite. The race started at 5:10 p.m.

Bill Brown took the early lead, walking the first mile in 8:26. "Hammond exercised great self-control in the matter of keeping down his pace in the early stages of the journey." **Jack Butler**, an elite walker who had held records, also contended for the lead.

A WALK THAT MADE A NEW WORLD'S RECORD

Finally, at around the 50 km (31 miles) mark, Hammond took the lead with a time of 5:11:47. From that point, he increased his lead over his opponents. He reached 50 miles in 8:36:31 with a mile lead and passed 100 miles at 18:08:50. He continued on with his strong swinging gait and won with an astonishing 131 miles, which was a world's walking best, and he smashed other walking records along the way. (**Charles Rowell** of England held the professional 24-hour record, running allowed, with 150 miles set in 1882 at Madison Square Garden.)

Middlesex Walking Club 24 Hour Track Walk, White City Stadium, London, 11-12 September 1908			
1. Tommy Hammond	White City	131 m 0580 yds	C10
2. H.W. Horton	Surrey WC	121 m 1645 yds	C5
3. F.J. Wakefield	Surrey WC	118 m 0301 yds	C6
4. C.M. Sampson	Polytechnic Harriers	117 m 1223 yds	C16
5. F.R. Leatherby	Middlesex WC	115 m 1613 yds	C17
6. Tommy Payne	Lancashire WC	108 m 0783 yds	C18
7. B.H. Warden	Polytechnic Harriers	108 m 0431 yds	C19
8. A. Ormrod	Lancashire WC	107 m 0644 yds	C20
9. F. Bland	Polytechnic Harriers	107 m 0344 yds	C15
10. J. Iles	Unattached-Wales	106 m 0785 yds	C21
11. Henry Swabey	Surrey WC	106 m 0743 yds	C13
12. Bob Gillespie	Middlesex WC	106 m 0154 yds	C22
13. H.J. Clark	Finchley Harriers	105 m 1504 yds	C23
14. George Lind	Polytechnic Harriers	104 m 0851 yds	C24
15. T.C. Habishaw	Queens Park	103 m 0465 yds	C25
16. J. Harper	Small Heath Harriers	100 m 0586 yds	C26
17. H.C. Taylor	Polytechnic Harriers	100 m 0586 yds	C27

At this race, seventeen walkers achieved 100 miles within 24 hours.

GREAT WALKING FEAT.

WORLD'S RECORDS FOR 24 HOURS BEATEN BY MILES.

"Those who knew best the record-breakers capabilities had predicted a remarkable performance and were not disappointed, as, although Hammond had more than one bad time, his superb courage and dogged determination enabled him to absolutely smash the then existing records."

Tom Payne

Thomas Payne (1882-1966) was born in South Shields, Durham, England. His father was a laborer at the Iron Foundry. By 1901, at the age of 19, Tom was a professional violinist, playing in the orchestra of Newcastle Theatre. He would walk 14 miles from his home in South Shields to work in order to save money. In 1906 he entered his first walking race, a 24-miler, and finished in second place.

Payne was a small man, 5 feet, 4 inches and only 112 pounds. He said, "Nature did not bless me with either undue length of body or length of limb, nor strength out of the ordinary, yet by hard, continuous

Tom Payne

training, I was able to overcome and defeat opponents who were much better gifted than me as regards build and strength."

Payne competed in more races and in 1907, started to win, beating established champions such as **Jack Butler**. Payne competed in the 1908 24-hour race in London and finished sixth with 108 miles, reaching 100 miles for the first time.

The Great 24 Hours' Race at the Stadium.

A merry group of famous pedestrians in the early stages of the great 24 hours' race won by Tom Payne. Names (from left) Jack Butler, 50 miles track record holder, G. H. Pateman, H. W. Horton, who finished 6th, and E. Parslow, who finished 7th.

1909 Blackheath Harriers' 24 Hour race

On September 17, 1909, another highly competitive 24-hour race was held at White City Stadium in London, England, open to all clubs. The entrants' field was huge, with fifty walkers who started at 5 p.m. in perfect weather. Payne competed along with the previous year's champion and world record holder, **Tommy Hammond**. Current and previous London to Brighton winners were also in the field. The early leaders included **Jack Butler**, **Bill Brown**, and **A. R. Edwards**.

The struggle for first place between W. Brown and T. Payne in the 16th hour of the race when both men had walked 84 miles. Payne took the lead shortly afterwards and eventually won by over 3 miles.

During the third hour, **H. V. L. Ross**, the current London to Brighton champion and record holder, put on a furious pace of more than seven m.p.h. and rapidly caught the leaders. "But he soon paid the penalty, for shortly before completing 25 miles he had to give up." Butler and Hammond also dropped out early, before 40 miles. "It was a curious coincidence that all of these competitors complained of cramp in the stomach." The leader, **J. Iles**, reached 51 miles is record time but "had shot his bolt" and after the next lap retired for more than an

Payne in the last hour

hour. He twice tried to get going again, but it didn't work, and he quit.

Brown took the lead and kept going at a steady gait. At twelve hours he reached 68 miles and was ahead of Hammond's 1908 record pace. But

Payne had the fastest pace on the track and during the 16th hour, took the lead.

Payne reached 100 miles in 18:08:55. He eventually won the race with 127 miles in 24 hours. An impressive 25 walkers reached 100 miles in less than 24 hours, the most in history up to that time in a single race.

In 1921 Payne performed a musical act where he burst through a large screen depicting the finish line at London to Brighton, dressed in a singlet and shorts, playing his violin. The AAA ruled that he broke amateur laws, and they suspended him from amateur racing for the next ten years. Past his prime, he did some racing in the 1930s and kept it up further until he was 77 years old. He died at the age of 84 in 1968.

The 1911 Centurion Club

The Surrey Walking Club's London to Brighton and back 100-miler expanded the popularization of reaching 100 miles within 24 hours in England. **E. R. "Bob" Gillespie** proposed that a society should be established to recognize the accomplishment. On May 11, 1911, at the Ship and Turtle public house in London, the "Brotherhood of Centurions" was established to recognize amateur walkers who had completed 100 miles in 24 hours.

James Edwin Fowler-Dixon, who was present at the organization meeting, was elected president, honored for his 100-mile walk in 1877. He was given the Centurion number of 1. Each Centurion received a number in order of the completion of the qualifying walk, and his name and number were entered into the minute book. They tried to go back in history a few years and award those who were believed to have achieved the milestone in the 1900s. Many were missed who succeeded in the late 1800s and professionals were not eligible and thus lost in their history.

The organization appointed London to Brighton and Back legend, **Tommy Hammond**, as the first secretary/treasurer and he was club captain for the next 36 years.

1912 London to Brighton and Back

The first race to qualify new members of the "Centurion Club" was the 1912 London to Brighton and Back race, held in September. **A. C. St. Norman,** of South Africa, entered. He had

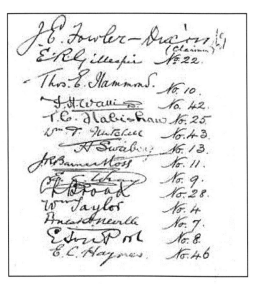

Original Centurion Committee

competed in the Olympic 10 km walking race (disqualified) and the Olympic marathon at the 1912 Olympic Games. There were only five walkers who started the 1912 Brighton double race. Three of them successfully qualified for the Centurions. "**St. Norman** showed fine judgement, and he is evidently suited by a long journey on the road. After allowing the leaders to force the pace, he came up at the 38th mile to lead." At the 100 km turnaround in Brighton, with 12:17:12, he had a 23-minute lead. He won by more than an hour over the others with a time of 21:18:45, making him the first new member of the Centurions since it had been established.

1914 London to Brighton and Back

The classic double Brighton was again held in 1914. The Surrey Walking Club finally opened up the race to non-members. "The Surrey Walking Club can certainly claim to be doing its best to further distance walking in as an unselfish a manner as possible. For the first time in the sport's history, every walker has an opportunity of testing his ability at the double journey without the necessity of previously becoming enrolled as a member." **E. F. Broad** won the 1914 race in 19:57:57 with the second-best time ever and won the "Hammond-Neville Trophy." This was the same man who won the first Stock Exchange London to Brighton walk in 1903. They held a veteran's division for those 45 and older. **George Hesketh** of Manchester Walking Club, age 48, won with 23:41:28.

26p.

1921, 1926, and 1929 London to Brighton and Back

The London to Brighton and Back was not staged post-World War I until 1921. "Races over the double journey are not so frequent." But there was plenty of interest in its return. Veteran, **Tommy Payne,** took the lead until the 100 km mark at the turnaround in

TOM PAYNE and SOME OF HIS PRIZES.

Brighton. The heat crushed him, and he dropped out. **Edgar C. Horton** took the lead at that point and won in 19:50:41. There were only two other finishers. Nine had dropped out along the way.

W. F. Baker

W. F. "Billy" Baker was an engineer who worked nights and had very recently taken up walking. He had an accident while cycling, and after recovering from a broken leg decided to instead take up walking. He joined the Queens Park Harriers Club.

In 1926, Baker won London to Brighton and Back in 18:05:51, setting a new course record, breaking Hammond's record that stood for twenty years. Horton placed second. Baker reached 100 miles in a walking 100-mile world record of 17:27:15.

For the 1929 edition, twenty-five walkers started. Baker went out fast and had the early lead at Big Ben (10 miles). He held onto that lead and won again with a time of 18:38:07, the third fastest time ever. He was "somewhat distressed" at the finish, but recovered. Fourteen others reach 100 miles in under 24 hours and qualified as Centurions.

London to Brighton and Back was held again a few more times in the next decades and held for the last time in 1967. Nineteen London to Brighton and Back races were held since 1902. A majority of the early British Centurions became members by virtue of completing this event. By 1930 there were 89 British Centurions and there were 302 by 1959. Yes, reaching 100 miles in less than 24 hours was alive and active during the first half of the 20th century, a historical fact that has been largely ignored or lost to the modern ultrarunner. For those keeping count, there were likely at least 700 finishes of 100 miles in less than 24 hours by the time the Great Depression arrived.

London to Brighton Running Race

In 1951, the London to Brighton *running* race was established by the Road Runners Club (RRC). By 1953, the race got the attention of leading long distance runners from other areas of the world, including those in America. Ultrarunning would largely be reestablished in America after World War II because long-distance runners, including **Ted Corbitt**, wanted to run London to Brighton. The London to

Ted Corbitt running London to Brighton

Brighton race, including its 100-mile version, has a hallowed place in ultrarunning history. It was discontinued in 2005 because of increased road traffic and difficulties finding enough volunteers.

CHAPTER EIGHT

Arthur Newton

In the 1920s, one of the greatest all-time British ultrarunners appeared, who made a serious impact on the forgotten 100-mile ultrarunning history before World War II. He was **Arthur Newton** of England, South Africa, and Rhodesia, and was a rare ultrarunning talent who had world-class ability in nearly all the ultrarunning distances from 50 km to 24-hours. Newton learned most of his serious running on a farm in remote Africa and was bold enough to step onto the world stage and beat everyone. His dominance in the early years of South Africa's Comrades Marathon (54 miles) helped the race get off the ground to become the oldest and largest ultramarathon in the world.

But Arthur Newton's best distance was 100 miles. With few 100-mile races to compete in during the 1920s, he resorted to taking part in highly monitored solo events to prove that a farmer from Africa was the best in the world, and he was. His 100-mile experiences will be shared, but also a good portion of his life story needs to be explained to understand the man, the ultrarunner, one of the greatest, **Arthur Newton**.

Early life

Arthur Francis Hamilton Newton (1883-1959) was born in Axbridge, Somerset, England. His father, **Henry Newton**, was at first a civil engineer and then went into religions ministry and served as a clerk in the Church of England. The family moved to Brighton, England, when Arthur was two years old. At age seven, he started to live in boarding schools full-time, first at Lady Matron School, and then as a teenager at Bedford School, a school for boys. He finished up in a private school in Banham, England. During his school years, he was

active in soccer, cricket and tennis but had no particular interest in running.

Durban, South Africa

After graduation in 1901, at the age of 18, he thought he would become a teacher. His father instead wanted him to be a clerk and sent him to South Africa to join two older brothers who were living in Durban. He tried the clerking career for a couple of years, but it was not for him, so he began teaching in the province of Natal. He played the piano, was an avid reader, and loved riding motorcycles. But he also was a regular smoker living a rather sedentary life. He explained, "I sacrificed the exercise necessary to a young man in order to dive deeper into metaphysics and allied subjects. Common sense soon came to the rescue, and I knew I should be able to make a better job of my mental work if I made certain of a healthy physique. So, I started a daily walk, whether I liked it or not."

The Running Teacher in South Africa

Newton began walking to his work and progressed to jogging distances up to six miles. "Sometimes people would stare quizzically at the eccentric Englishman running down the road." He became bothered by these reactions, so moved his

Drakensberg Mountain Range

exercise during the early hours when few people were out. He began very fit and showed his abilities to the schoolboys he was teaching. He once organized a 300-mile round trip to the Drakensberg mountain range that involved bike riding and hiking.

Howick

Newton's first running race took place when he was age 24 in February 1908. It was a 11-mile "go as you please" race in the small rural town of Howick. The town was the site of a sad British internment camp where many women and children died a few

years earlier during the Anglo-Boer War. He was one of eight runners who took part, and he finished in fourth place with a time of about 90 minutes. He soon started to win some races. On a long excursion to the mountains, he ran out of cigarettes and was convinced by a friend to start using a pipe instead.

In 1909, his father found him a job as a tea planter in Ceylon (Sri Lanka) where the family had previously lived when his father was working as a civil engineer. So, he returned to England. By the time he arrived, the opportunity was gone and at age 26, he was without permanent work. He joined the Thames Hare and Hounds cross-country club, the oldest such club in the world. He finished third in his first

race and continued to excel in others. For years Newton would wear the cross-country "X" on his racing jerseys.

He said, "Several weeks at home, just idling around proved too much, and I told my father that I wanted to get back to South Africa. He said he had guessed as much, and perhaps I had better go. So back to Natal I was sent and accepted a position as a tutor on a farm near Harding.

South African Farmer

By 1911, Newton became a farmer. He bought 1,350 acres from the government with the help of his father. "I had a desperate struggle to

make both ends meet. Assistance from home helped me to tide over the worst and at last there came a time when I had learnt enough to be able to get along on my own." He worked hard in an environment of solitude and also did some cross-country running. His farm initially was ten miles from the nearest road and only connected by footpaths. He would frequently run to and from his mailbox several miles away from his house. Black indigenous Zulu lived on "his" land and paid some rent.

During World War I, starting in 1914, Newton desired to serve and was assigned to a detachment called the Natal Light Horse fighting against white Boers who had sided with the Germans. He became a military messenger and used his own motorcycle to deliver messages. "I

offered to take my motorcycle at my own expense, as I realized I was far more likely to be useful as a dispatch rider than anything else, being a competent and experienced motorcyclist."

When Newton's service ended, he returned to his farm in 1918 and found it in a state of neglect being grazed by Zulu cattle herders. Grass fires had destroyed about two-thirds of his grazing land. Newton wanted to convert his land to be more profitable, to

Cotton field in South Africa

cultivate cotton and tobacco. But the Zulu tenants on his land objected changing their centuries-old lifestyle. They did not want to become farm laborers earning wages, and his tenants would disagree with him about nearly everything. On top of that, it became increasingly difficult to collect rent from them. It was a clash of culture, race, and politics.

The government started relocating more blacks to live in the area around Newton's farm and with current conditions in the country, the Zulu did not trust the white Englishman. Newton also did not trust the government or the Zulu to help find a way to make his farm work.

He asked the government to exchange his farm for another farm in a "white area", but the Department of Native Affairs refused. This led to a standoff between the farmer Newton and the South African government. He realized it would be impossible for him to become a successful cotton farmer and find willing local laborers.

Decision to Become a Serious Runner

Newton became convinced that the reason the government was treating him poorly was because he was unknown to them. He decided that he needed to make himself famous. "Evidently, I should have to make my name and the circumstances known to the public. I should then be in a position to show my fellow citizens how settlers should be safe-guarded." He came up with a bizarre idea. He decided that his route to be famous was to become an elite runner. He believed, "Genuine amateur athletics were about as wholesome as anything on earth. Any man who made a really notable name at such would always be given a hearing by the public. I took up long-distance running solely with the object of focusing public attention on the treatment to which I had been subjected." He set his sights to win the new annual

54-mile Comrades Marathon that ran between Durban and Pietermaritzburg in South Africa. In 1922, Comrades would be run for the second year.

In January 1922, at the age of 38, Newton seriously thought he could win Comrades with less than five months' serious training after nearly ten years without consistent training. He said, "Knowing through my studies that any average man could do as well as other average men if he were really determined and was in possession of an average physique – and with the Comrades Marathon already in existence – I decided that what with my age, it would be quicker and probably easier to achieve publicity through long-distance running than by any other methods."

The Comrades Marathon

The first Comrades Marathon was held on "Empire Day" on May 24, 1921. It was founded by **Vic Clapham** (1886-1962), a train driver from Durban. The 52-mile London to Brighton races before World War I had inspired Clapham, he and wanted to create a similar race as a living memorial to fallen soldiers of the war. The inaugural Comrades

race with 34 runners, most of them former infantrymen, received good newspaper press coverage and Newton noticed.

Vic Clapham

Bill Rowan

For the early Comrades Marathon years, runners were followed by friends on bicycles or automobiles to provide support. Farmers holding picnic parties along the route also handed out food to the runners. The first year was won by a farmer, **Bill Rowan**, in 8:59. Sixteen runners finished by the 12-hour limit on the mostly dirt road course.

Training for 1922 Comrades

In preparing for the 1922 Comrades race, Newton, age 38, established a serious training program using any literature he could find on the subject. He knew that he had to be able to run 54 miles at roughly a nine-minute mile pace to win. This ultra-distance would be much further than his cross-country races of previous years and he believed he was old, so thought it would be hard on him.

Because farming had been rendered useless to him, he devoted most of his hours each day for five months in training. He knew that the previous winner, **Bill Rowan** had trained doing 20-mile runs on his farm. Newton said, "My condition was quite reasonably good. I could walk 15-20 miles in a day over rough country without becoming exhausted, so I was surprised to find that two miles of running were altogether beyond me. After that I was so abominably stiff that I cut out running for a day or two and walked instead."

He finally admitted to himself that if he was to succeed, he would have to put aside his smoking after 20 years of the habit. Going cold turkey was too difficult, and he finally decided to allow himself two pipes a day, including a post-run pipe as a reward for hard training. His runs worked up to 25 miles and he dropped his weight by ten pounds to 132 pounds.

1922 Comrades Marathon

There were 89 runners on May 24, 1922, who start at 6 a.m. for the long run from Durban to Pietermaritzburg, the "up" version of the course in the Drakensberg Mountains. They were cheered on by a crowd of 2,000 people.

The mayor of Durban fired the starting pistol, and they were off, followed by helpers in cars, rickshaws, bicycles and motorbikes. Newton was ridiculed by some spectators for holding back his pace and being in the back of the pack. But soon he moved up and passed runners. By 20 miles, he was passing undertrained runners who were walking. He was mid-pack by the halfway point and still not worried about the front-runners.

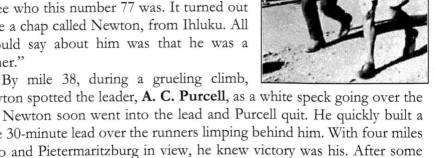

By mile 30, he passed the previous year's winner, **Bill Rowan**, who went out too fast and was battling cramps. Only three other men were ahead. The race director, **Vic Clapham**, received word that an unknown runner "77" was among the front-runners. He said, "There was a scramble for programmes to see who this number 77 was. It turned out to be a chap called Newton, from Ihluku. All I could say about him was that he was a farmer."

By mile 38, during a grueling climb, Newton spotted the leader, **A. C. Purcell**, as a white speck going over the top. Newton soon went into the lead and Purcell quit. He quickly built a large 30-minute lead over the runners limping behind him. With four miles to go and Pietermaritzburg in view, he knew victory was his. After some brandy at a hotel, he attacked the last stretch.

At the Sports Ground, he ran on the track and thousands cheered him on as he ran the last stretch around the track. He said, "At last I saw the tape ahead and ran to it in a tumultuous roar and cheering from all sides to get a handshake from the city mayor."

Newton finished in 8:40, nearly 20 minutes faster than the first year's winner. A crowd lifted him off his feet and paraded him on their shoulders off the field. Reporters followed and photographed. His friends took him away to recover. He told reporters that he did not think he would try to run that far again. "After all, I'm 39 and getting on in years."

1922 Comrades Marathon finish

Full time Runner

Newton competed again at the 1923 Comrades, this time running the "down" course. He dominated and reached the finish faster than anyone thought possible. The officials were not yet prepared for his arrival. "One man, however, happened to spot me shortly before I reached the Sports Ground and diving through a broken fence as a short cut, was able to gather another man inside and arrive at the finishing post just in time to hold up the tape and read the watches." He finished in 6:56, nearly an hour ahead of the second-place runner. Newton's fame started to spread to England.

But the fame was not enough to produce the results he hoped for. He said, "I took stock of my position, felt that I had by no means established myself as a well-known public character, and decided that more training work, even harder work, had to be the order of the day. It looked as though nothing less than world's records would bring me the publicity I knew was required." His weekly mileage was consistently more than 100 miles and reached as much as 253 miles in a week.

50-mile World Record

In 1923, Newton wanted to go after the amateur 50-mile world record of 6:13 but didn't want to run on a track because he thought that the monotony of running circles on a track was awful. So instead, a 25-mile length of dirt road was measured on the road from Pietermaritzburg to Durban, the same road used by the Comrades Marathon. He knew every inch of the hilly road and felt confident on it.

Newton's attempt was made on June 29, 1923, just five weeks after Comrades. He started at 7 a.m. in a cool mist and said, "I was glad to get to work, though more than a trifle nervous." The official cars had to stay well behind or in front of him to avoid kicking up large clouds of dust. To counter skepticism about the measurement with automobile odometers, he surprised officials by running an extra 200 yards at the 25-mile turnaround.

At the finish, a large crowd gathered, and the police kept a lane open for him to run for the last half mile. He succeeded and broke all world's fastest-known 50-mile times with 5:53:05. The previous fastest time was **George Cartwright's** professional mark of 5:55:04, set indoors back in 1887. But weeks later, he received a letter from London from the Amateur Athletics Association stating that since he ran on the road rather than on a measured track, that his time would not be recognized as a world's best. The Brits obviously wouldn't accept any record not

achieved on their soil and not by one of their runners. **Fowler-Dixon**, the author of the letter, suggested that Newton come to England to run London to Brighton. The British sporting press scoffed at the idea of accepting a world record on a dusty road in Africa. Despite all the monitoring and verification that was put in place, even today the performance would not be recognized as a world record because it was not part of a competitive race. Nevertheless, his record happened. For 1923, Newton ran a staggering 9,168 miles, an unprecedented total.

50-milers in England

Newton wanted to prove to British skeptics that his 50-mile record was valid. In England, he adjusted to training on busy English roads. The harder road surfaces gave his joints problems. He had to reduce his weekly mileage to about 120 miles until he felt better. Arrangements were made for a solo London to Brighton conducted by representatives of the AAA.

Newton attempted the London to Brighton course on October 3, 1924. The current London to Brighton course record holder, **Len Hurst,** (1871-1937) followed along in one of the timekeeper automobiles, giving him encouragement. Newton proved his doubters

wrong and finished in 6:11:04, which was faster than the course record by about 23 minutes. He passed through the 50-mile mark in 5:57:48, slower than his time in South Africa.

Not satisfied with his performance, wanting to break six hours on the course, Newton, age 41, repeated the run the following month on November 13, 1924, in bad weather that was preceded by 36 hours of continuous rain.

Newton Breaks World's Record

Newton had to splash through many unavoidable puddles along the way but pushed hard and finished with a time of 5:53:43, and a 50-mile split time of 5:38:42 crushing his world's best 50-mile time. An excited crowd at the Aquarium in Brighton roared. News of his amazing accomplishment was published widely across the world and thought to be a record never to be broken. But the British Amateur Athletic Association (AAA), as expected, announced that neither of his London to Brighton runs would be officially recognized as records because they were solo runs not accomplished in a race which greatly annoyed Newton. They could have told him that before his attempts, which they officiated at. They seemed to be doing everything possible to keep Newton out of their record books. But the world knew it happened.

Back to South Africa

Newton left England on November 27, 1924, sailing on the *SS Bendigo* bound for South Africa. With changes politically in the government while he was away, all promises made to him were gone. Unable to pay the interest on his mortgage, he sold his farm. Appeals for help

from the new government went nowhere, as they considered him an English settler who was a vocal government critic. Newton decided to leave South Africa and go to the nearby country of Rhodesia, which was a British colony.

In 1925, Newton won Comrades for the fourth straight year, lowering the "down" record to 6:24:54. As a final farewell, on July 25, 1925, he ran a solo "down" Comrades route in his best time ever, 6:14:30.

Just 36 hours later, Newton left Pietermaritzburg, where he had lived for seven months. He did not want to make a public fuss, so left privately one night with the quest to walk 770 miles to Rhodesia. He was poverty-stricken, had been living on the kind charity of a hotel owner, and knew that the arrangement could not continue. He would go into exile. He wrote, "Six years of a real sporting fight had changed me from an active and prosperous farmer to an energetic and all-but-penniless tramp."

The South African news soon noticed that he was gone, initially worried about him, and speculated about why he disappeared until several days later he was seen on the road. After a few days, he accepted offers to ride in cars and receive kind room and board. It took him nearly three months to arrive in Rhodesia.

When competing, Newton started to wear on his jersey "Natal" to honor his former long-time South African home and "Rhodesia," his new home. He first worked as a foreman at a mine.

First 100-miler - Rhodesia

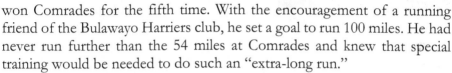

In 1927, after two years in Rhodesia, Newton went back to South Africa and won Comrades for the fifth time. With the encouragement of a running friend of the Bulawayo Harriers club, he set a goal to run 100 miles. He had never run further than the 54 miles at Comrades and knew that special training would be needed to do such an "extra-long run."

Newton knew that in order to accomplish an exceptional 100-mile time, he needed other runners to compete against. He could not find any willing competitors to race 100 miles, so for his attempt, he recruited a relay of six runners from the Harriers club. "As they were all men whose normal distances were between one and ten miles, they were taking on just about as big a job as I was, and they knew it."

For his 100-mile run, he chose a flat 100-mile road course from Gweru to Bulawayo in today's Zimbabwe with only about 1,500 feet of climbing along the way. They carefully measured the course using a measuring wheel and Newton added a quarter mile just to make sure he reached 100 miles.

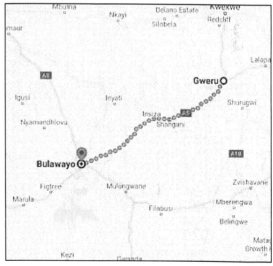

On July 11, 1927, at 6:10 a.m., Newton set off to run 100 miles for the first time after eating a large breakfast. He gave the relay runner a head-start so as not to distract him. He said, "It was dark at first but an official car about fifty yards behind me flood-lighted the road which had quite a decent dirt surface, and I ambled along at a serenely easy seven miles per hour."

Between miles 25-45, the temperature rose to an uncomfortable level. He stopped to cool off in a roadside pool. At the half-way point, he stopped at a hotel for a pre-ordered lunch. "My fodder was soup, chicken and vegetables, and fruit pie. Twelve minutes later, I was on the road again, climbing a gentle gradient on my way to Bulawayo." On the road, he was fueled by hot tea from thermos flasks.

After 70 miles, the sun began to set. He wrote, "The car floodlighted the road while I crept steadily on, feeling that there was still a chance that I might reach the end, though I was in for a real bad time." He drank piping hot tea every three miles or so and pressed on at a steady ten-minute-mile pace. He said, "Every nerve and fiber seemed to be crying for rest."

A crowd of 300 greeted him at the finish at King's Grounds. He had beaten his relay team by a few minutes and finished in 14:43:00, which was believed to be an <u>amateur</u> 100-mile world record. He had indeed significantly improved the fastest known <u>amateur</u> time of 16:07:43, held by **Sidney Hatch**. The world's best 100-mile time overall was still 13:26:30, set by **Charles Rowell** in 1882, indoors at Madison Square Garden.

At the finish, Newton placed his feet in a bath of hot water, smoked a pipe and drank some drinks. He recalled, "I found it difficult even to talk and answer the many questions fired at me." His 100-mile run was not recognized by the British Amateur Athletic Association because of doubts over the expertise of the

CLAIMS NEW MARK FOR 100 MILE RUN

Arthur Newton, South African Marathon Runner, Completes Race.

Rhodesian officials. This was a disappointment to him, but not a surprise. He wanted Rhodesia to claim a world record.

THE BULAWAYO CHRONICLE

NEWTON TO RUN IN ENGLAND

Skeptics in England made noise again, which bothered Newton's friends in Rhodesia. "The improvement on the record was so unbelievable to many of these good people of Rhodesia that they, there and then, decided to take steps to send me to England to attempt a better time under more favourable conditions. Feeling that I now knew something of what was needed for this type of race, I willingly agreed."

Funds were raised to allow him to travel to England. "I wanted to make good the time or perhaps even beat it, on some well-known course such as the Bath Road. As I was more than willing to do anything I could to show my appreciation of all the kindness I had met with in this splendid country (Rhodesia), it wasn't long before I found myself sailing to England." He left during the late fall of 1927 and turned professional, having an eye on perhaps entering **C.C. Pyle's** upcoming 1928 race across America. "On the boat coming over, he kept fit by running twenty miles on the decks almost every day." When running at night, he wore rubber shoes so he wouldn't disturb the other passengers.

100 miles on the Bath Road

Joe Binks of *News of the World,* sponsored arrangements for Newton to make a 100-mile record attempt in England on Bath

ATHLETICS.

World's Record-Holder in London.

Road (A4) from Box to Hyde Park Corner. The old Bath Road was a historic route marched by Roman Centurions between the two famous cities. It also had been used by stagecoaches and the professional pedestrians of the past century.

In 1886, "The Bath Road Club" was formed for cyclists which conducted races as long as 100 miles on the road. By 1891, the fastest known time wheeling 100 miles on the road on an out-and-back course was 5:59:11. By 1925, the record time had been lowered to 4:43:29 by **A. Harbour.**

F. H. Grubb, who made record time of 4 hrs. 50 min. 49l sec. in the Bath Road " 100."

·A·F·H·NEWTON·

In December 1927, because there were no longer skilled 100-mile runners in England, Binks recruited a four-man relay team to run against Newton on Bath Road and made sure the press and public were aware of the event. The relay runners were **E. G. Hubert, R. Norton, H. G. Wickington,** and **M. J. Terrett.** Newton hoped to break 14 hours. The weather leading up to the run was poor with much snow. Newton recalled, "I remember one day when I gave up training entirely. I had managed to flounder part of the way through a 4-5-foot drift that blanketed the path from the house for 50 yards or more." Four days before the 100-miler, rain came, which resulted in severe flooding.

Newton started his 100-mile journey on January 7, 1928, at 2 a.m., from Bear Inn in the village of Box, near Bath. Olympic sprinter, **Harold Abrahams** (depicted in the movie *Chariots of Fire)* was at the start to watch Newton begin. Despite the early morning start, many men on bicycles followed after him. The snow was mostly gone, but some fierce winds with rain made the going rough. Still,

Start of 100-miler with first relay runner

many people in each town came out to cheer loudly and watch the spectacle.

About his running style, it was observed, "He glides along, feet no more than two or three inches off the ground, and noiseless. Not flat footed, but more on his heels, and astonishing silent breathing."

He kept pace with the relay runner who was only going the first 25 miles (2:53), but then he struggled, feeling ill. By 40 miles, his illness was pretty evident to his crew, but he was still ahead of schedule. Hot tea helped, and he stopped for ten minutes to eat a breakfast of minced beef. The sickness continued and the relay team had a big lead. He tried drinking his "magic drink" often but could not take in any solid food.

It was reported, "His lower half was by now filthy from the muddy water splashed up by his own feet, and he became wetter still when going through Maidenhead, parts of which were completely underwater." They had put temporary wooden walkways in place over the water which Newton used. "At seventy miles Newton was sick, and his progress over the last thirty miles was away doggedly though obviously distressed"

Flood in Maidenhead

Coming into London, some enthusiastic spectators slapped him hard on the back as he passed, sometimes spinning him completely around. Soon, he was able to speed up. By 12 hours, he reached 87 miles and was accompanied by many bicyclists. His official support car broke down. A newsman omnibus came to the rescue and took on the task to crew him.

At mile 95, Newton called out, "How far?" He was mobbed by the crowd which the police tried to hold back. Dozens of noisy kids ran along close behind him. They received irritated looks from Newton, worried that they would clip his heels. At about 4:30 p.m. he approached the finish at Hyde Park. Movie men filmed, and the road was packed with people, cars and horses.

"Before reaching the official finish line, he appeared to falter. Two or three enthusiasts then seized him but shook them off and ran on to cross the line in 14:22:10, breaking his previous amateur world record. He was disoriented and swept up, taken to the nearby hospital. The crowd chanted, 'We want Newton.' Some tried to storm the hospital entrance to see him. After ten minutes of recovery, he came out the doors and thanked everyone."

Later, he explained, "I was pleased enough to get through it in twenty minutes less time than the 100 in Rhodesia, but that was all that could be said about it." He had never experienced such severe stomach trouble. He wore wool clothes to keep him warm, but they caused him to sweat profusely during the day. He knew that he could run 100 miles much faster. Congratulations poured in, including from the chancellor of Rhodesia.

It should be noted that the Bath Road from Box to Hyde Park Corner is 100.25 miles, according to the engraved milestone, in Box. However, it is believed that the road in Newton's time was almost certainly short of 100 miles.

The Bunion Derby

Newton signed up to run C. C. Pyle's 1928 race across America, Los Angeles to New York, which the press coined, "The Bunion Derby." Newton, age 44, was the pre-race favorite. After a week in the race conducted in daily stages, he was in the lead. But on the 15th day he quit because of a severely sprained ankle and a strained leg. Newton ran again in the 1929 version of the Bunion Derby, New York, to Los Angeles, but in Indiana, while in 9th place, a car struck him, and he dropped out with a dislocated shoulder.

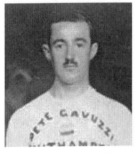

Peter Gavuzzi

Ollie Wanttinen

Two runners who ran in the Bunion Derby, later ran solo 100-miles. **Peter Gavuzzi** of the U.K., who barely finished second in the 1929 Bunion Derby with a controversial finish. He ran a solo road 100-miler during August 1935 from Buffalo, New York to Toronto, Canada. His time was 15:25:34.

Ollie Wanttinen, of Finland, the 5'2" 90-pound "Mighty Mite," ran a solo 100-miler in Helsingfor, Finland (now Helsinki) on May 24, 1934, with a time of 15:13:33.

24-hour World Record

In 1931, Newton organized his own event in Hamilton, Ontario, Canada, to attempt to break the 24-hour long-time world record of 150 miles set by **Charles Rowell** back in 1882. With the Great Depression raging around the world, Canada was initially affected less, and many of the elite ultrarunners

went there to compete. The 24-hour race was an invitation-only event. America's best, Johnny Salo could not make it, but other Bunion Derby veterans, including **Paul "Hardrock" Simpson** competed.

Newton put together the event similar to the Madison Square Garden events of the former century. It was held in Hamilton's ice-hockey and skating arena. He hired an orchestra to play non-stop and boxers and wrestlers to perform inside the track. Cyclists were hired as warm-up acts. The press said the event would include "fights, hikes and bikes." The wooden track covered with felt and paper was tiny, 13 laps to a mile, in an odd square shape with banked corners. Track etiquette asked that the slower competitors step aside as a faster runner passed from behind.

On April 4, 1931, the indoor 24-hour event took place. They ran surrounded by mostly empty seats. **Mike McNamara** from Australia reached 100 miles first in 14:09:45 and then decided to quit. Newton had hoped that McNamara would continue, giving him someone to battle for the 24 hours win. Two others were still running but far behind. He wrote, "Quite unexpectedly, I was left alone to try for the 24-hour title." He tried to not to look at the clock and pushed ahead at about 8.5-minute-mile pace. As he got close to the 150-mile world record that was set by **Charles Rowell** in 1882, he increased speed up to an astonishing six-minute-mile pace.

When time was called, Newton set a new world 24-hour record of 152 miles, 540 yards, circling the arena 1,926 times. His record would last for 22 years until broken by South African **Wally Hayward**.

Arthur Newton Breaks 24-Hour Running Record

The event was a financial disaster and Newton lost a bundle. "It takes courage for a man to run 24 hours, especially when he knows that instead of being rewarded for his efforts, he must lose money."

1933 100-miler on Bath Road

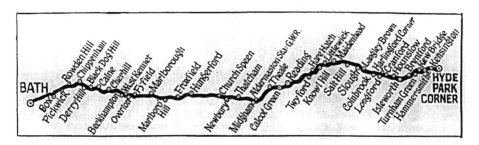

As his 50th birthday approached in 1933, Newton wanted to try to break the 100-mile world record again before retiring. He felt that 100 miles was his best distance and wanted to run it on his birthday, May 20, 1933. It was reported, "He will run for nothing but the glory of the sport and will make this his final race."

For training in March 1933, he ran an amazing 1,084 miles, including a 270-mile week. But he postponed his race when invited to run in France for a large sum of money. Later, he ran the 100-mile run in the heat of the summer on July 1, 1933. He covered the first 50 miles on Bath Road in 5:56:30, 45 minutes ahead of schedule. But a mile or two later, the wheels started to fall off, and he began limping. He reached 60 miles in 7:15:30, which he was told was a new record. But Newton's Achilles hurt, and his stomach went south in the heat. He reached 74 miles in 9:41:50, almost an hour ahead of schedule but was on a downward spiral.

Newton refused to think of giving up after covering more than 80 miles. He reached 85 miles in 11:24:30 during mid-afternoon, the hottest time of the day with temperatures in the 80s. Soon he started to sway, and his crew insisted that he quit because of sunstroke. He had no choice, and it was the first time he ever quit a record attempt. He reached 86 miles in 11:33:00. After recovering, he agreed that his health was being put at serious risk.

Unwisely, Newton decided to try 100 miles again just three weeks later on July 22, 1933. He was desperate to "make amends." His Achilles became inflamed with a week to go, but he was determined. He started at 3:00 a.m., again at Bear Inn in Box. More than 100 people were at the start. Things went well early, but by mile 25, he was noticeably limping. By mile 30, it was clear that he wouldn't make it and could not run through it. He was very distressed and close to tears and quit again. He said, "I was quite shocked at the disaster and at having given the officials so much work and travel for nothing." His injuries would last for a long time and limped for the next ten months. He used the downtime for coaching and writing.

1934 100-miler on Bath Road

Finally recovered from his injuries, Newton wanted to try for the 100-mile record one last time in 1934. July 20th was the day chosen. He wrote, "I went to Bath once more. It was neck or nothing this time, and I knew it. Already 51 years old, I couldn't expect to keep up 700-800 miles a month on my feet indefinitely." He had run about 95,000 miles during the past 13 years as a runner. Friends came from as far as Africa to watch.

At the end of his run, the time was 14:11:30. Historian, Andy Milroy explained, "This irritated Newton because at the 24-hour indoor race in 1931, **Mike McNamara** of Australia had reached 100 miles in 14:09:45. Because the Bath Road was believed to be 100.25 miles, Newton claimed that for 100 miles his time would have been five minutes faster, 14:06:00, because of the extra quarter mile." (The Bath Road was laid out a century earlier, because of changes, the entire distance was actually short of 100.25 miles, and short of 100 miles.)

But it also disappointed Newton that he did not break 14 hours. He knew at 51, his age was now a slowdown factor. He knew that would be his last 100-miler. He said, "There remained only one useful alternative, and that was to put my experience at the disposal of other athletes so that they could carry on where I had left off." Others did come in future years and broke his Bath Road 100-mile record.

News spread around the world about his accomplishment. One journalist remarked, "A committee of medical men should go into a huddle over Arthur Newton and find what he eats, what he drinks, and all about his

A Marvel at Fifty

Britisher Runs 100 Miles in 14 Hours, 6 Minutes, Then Asks for Smoke

habits of living. There must be a valuable lesson in all this for mankind in general."

Retirement From Competitive Running

Later in 1934, Newton announced his retirement from competitive running. He had run more

Bunion Derby Vet Will Slow Down

than 100,000 miles during his career. Even though he no longer raced, he continued to give back to the sport through coaching, writing books, and helping other ultrarunners break records. An old friend, **Walter George**, who once held the mile world record, wrote, "Newton is unquestionably the most phenomenal distance runner the world has ever known. No man in the past has succeeded in doing what he has done, and it may be centuries before his records are surpassed."

By the late 1940s, Newton was still running for pleasure. At age 65 he had cut his daily runs down to less than ten miles. He had taken up cycling and would often ride long distances to Wales and Scotland. He experienced health problems with his eyesight and high blood pressure, which began to limit what he could do. In 1951 he was a driving force for reviving the London to Brighton run. They still revered him in South Africa, a legend of the Comrades Marathon.

By 1955, Newton's health was seriously failing, including increased blindness, making any running impossible. At age 72, he could still go out for long walks. He received many visitors from people wishing to spend time with one of the all-time greatest distance runners of the world. Arrangements were made for him to visit South Africa and Rhodesia one last time. He greatly enjoyed

Runner Dies

Hillingdon, England, Sept. 7 — (Reuters) — Arthur Newton, one of the finest long-distance runners of all time, died in a hospital here today. He was 76. After taking up marathon running at the age of 40, he broke amateur and professional world running records for every distance from 29 to 150 miles.

the trip. By the late 1950s, Newton was still walking as much as 90 miles per week. During the summer of 1959, his time was coming to an end after suffering a minor stroke. He died on September 7, 1959, at Hillingdon Hospital at age 76.

Newton soon became forgotten by most. In South Africa, he still is referred by some as "Greatheart" in recognition of his many donations of trophies to deserving causes. He is remembered the most for being a founding father of the Comrades Marathon.

At the course's halfway point near Drummond, there is a landmark that runners look for called, "Arthur's Seat." It was known to be Newton's favorite resting spot during his five Comrades wins. A Comrades legend is told about Arthur's Seat that if a runner leaves a flower, tips their cap and says, "Good morning Mr. Newton," that they would experience a strong second half of the race.

CHAPTER NINE

Hardy Ballington

Hardy Robert Ballington (1912-1974) was born July 14, 1912, in South Africa. He became known as the "second Newton" and a "human machine." His father was **Edward William Ballington** and his mother **Kate Elizabeth Sims**, both born in England. He was one of five brothers and two sisters, the third eldest child, one of twins.

1881 Census record from Staffordshire showing Hardy's father, Edward Ballington as a child in his family. His mother was a sergeant's wife.

Hardy's father died in 1921 and his mother three years later giving birth to her eleventh child. The six living minor children, including young eleven-year-old Hardy became orphans and were put in the care of the Society for Protections of Child Life in Cape Town, South Africa.

He joined the scouts, giving him structure to his unsteady life. In 1929, he traveled to England as a scout patrol leader as part of a large South African patrol to the World Scout Jamboree at Arrowe Park, Upton, near Birkenhead, in England. It was attended by scouting founder **Robert Baden-Powell**.

At age 18, in 1930, Ballington had become overweight and unhealthy. After spending some time in the hospital, he took up running for his health. After attending night classes, he would run so no one would see him. Initially, he had no intention of competing in races. But in 1931, he entered his first marathon in Pietermaritzburg, where he finished in fourth place.

Success at Comrades

By 1932, at the age of 20, Ballington emerged as a promising new runner. In the early 1930s, a veteran runner, **Vernon Jones**, spotted young Ballington on a training run. He noticed he had huge calf muscles and said to Ballington, "Young man, you ought to take part in the Comrades Marathon." Ballington set his sights on running Comrades (54 miles). He did, in 1932, and finished in a surprising fourth place with 8:01:14. He then won the Durban Athletic Club Marathon in 3:00:04. But he soon put his concentration on the ultra-distances and believed he could win Comrades.

He would become one of the greatest of all the Comrades champions.

In 1933, Ballington joined a field of 85 runners in the 13th edition of Comrades. The weather was poor with rain and freezing

wind. By the half-way point, he was in third place. He fell behind some as he stopped to change his shoes. But soon he took charge of the race and passed the leaders climbing Botha's Hill and quickly extended his lead. "Wearing a sweater as protection against the rain and cold, Ballington forged ahead in the closing stages. There was no stopping him. Comrades had a new great champion." He became only the second runner after Newton to break the seven-hour barrier with a time of 6:50:37.

Ballington's success continued, as **Arthur Newton** trained him remotely from England. He won Comrades again in 1934 and 1936. During the depression era, he became known as the world's greatest ultra-distance runner.

To England

With Ballington's success, he recalled, "Since 1933, I had shown steady improvement in my running, and now in 1937 the Durban Athletic Club members considered I had attained world class and decided to send me to England to run in the London to Brighton race, and also the 100 miles from Bath to London."

"On arrival in England. I was met by the great **Arthur Newton**. It was our first meeting, although we had corresponded for several years. Arthur Newton introduced me to **Joe Binks**, the Sports Editor of *The News of the World*. Joe Binks wrote in his paper that South Africa had sent a schoolboy over to do a man's job and was not impressed. However, this made me all the more determined, and I moved into the country to concentrate on my training."

Ballington's London to Brighton Record

By going to England, Ballington skipped running Comrades and instead wanted to go after Arthur Newton's 50 and 100-mile records that he set in England. Newton was the driving force behind Ballington's attempts that were sponsored by *News of the World*. Newton paid special attention to Ballington, escorting him by bike on his training runs. He logged an astonishing 1,100 miles on training runs in one month.

Newton and Ballington

RECORD RUN TO BRIGHTON

A MARGIN OF ONE SECOND

At the special May 22, 1937, London to Brighton running race, eight runners including Ballington competed. The 24-year-old ran steady, to his own schedule, crewed by Newton. "He maintained practically the same pace throughout. A head wind and rain made conditions extremely difficult for the great part of the way, but he showed no signs of fatigue and finished with a very strong sprint." After he crossed the finish line, it was announced that he had beaten Newton's 1924 course record by a minute and a half. But then a confusing announcement was communicated that he had failed by 12 seconds. But later it was determined because of different finishing points, Ballington's run was about 100 yards further and they adjusted his official time to 5:53:42, beating Newton's time by one second, a record held for the next 16 years.

Ballington's 100-mile World Record

Next, Ballington wanted to go after Newton's 100-mile record on the Bath Road. He wrote, "I moved to the West Country to train for the 100 miles from Bath to London. During the month of June, the weather was perfect, and I covered over 1,400 miles in training (46 miles per day). I stayed in Newbury for a while and then decided I would like to move nearer to Bath, so arranged to stay with people near Marlborough. You can imagine my surprise when I turned up at the residence, to be told that there was no bath in the house and if I wanted a bath, I could use a tub in the living room once a week. You bet I decided to stay in Newbury."

Ballington made his attempt on July 3, 1937, at 3:30 a.m. The day turned out to be very hot. The heat was so extreme in London that day, that the Wimbledon tennis finals was delayed for two hours. The starting point as usual, was at the Bear Inn, in the small village of Box in Wiltshire, on the A4 route to Hyde Park Corner in London, 100 miles away.

Fletcher handling Ballington. McNamara walking on left while Newton watches

Ballington, crewed by **Arthur Newton** and also by 100-mile great, **Mike McNamara**, and a young man from Durban, G.C.M. Fletcher. Fletcher would jump out of one of the accompanying cars, determine what drinks Ballington needed, then return to the car. The car then drove 100 yards ahead, so the drink could be prepared and delivered. His crew had challenges. "Newton had to deal with an unfortunate episode in a tea shop, where the haughty proprietor would only serve tea in cups for drinking on the premises, and wouldn't allow Newton to fill a flask to take outside to thirsty Ballington."

Ballington crushed Newton's time, finishing in 13:21:19, which also beat **Charles Rowell's** 1882 world record time of 13:26:30. He wrote afterwards, "I received a tremendous reception on arrival in Hyde Park and broke the amateur world record by over an hour."

For the following week, both Ballington and Newton held daily public appearances at the *News of the World's* sports department. For Ballington's impressive accomplishments, far away in America, he was recognized at "The Sportsman of 1937" by the Helms world trophy organization in California. It took them 20 years  to track down Ballington to send him the trophy.

Early Running Retirement

Ballington returned to South Africa and won at Comrades again in 1938. He was 25 years old. Historian, **Andy Milroy** wrote, "Athletics was generally thought of as being part of childhood. By continuing on to run at such an 'older' age, Ballington was perhaps threatening his professional career as a clerk at Durban City Council. He had invested a lot of time in night school to gain that position."

Through the challenging World War II times of the 1940s, not much is known about Ballington's running efforts, but in 1947, after the war, Ballington won the Comrades Marathon for the fifth and final time at the age of 35. He went on to be a travel agent and by 1966 had flown around the world six times, visiting the major cities of the world. In 1969, Comrades established the "Hardy Ballington Trophy" for the first novice runner to finish the race.

In 1974, Hardy Ballington died in his sleep at the age of 61.

CHAPTER TEN

Various 100 Mile Attempts 1900-1935

The Tarahumara

There was a place in the world where ultra-distance running never took a vacation. Running 100 miles or more was ingrained into the culture of the Tarahumara, a civilization of about 30,000 people who seemingly were untouched by the modern world. They

A RACE OF FOOT RUNNERS

The Tarahumaras Indiana Travel Long Distances Quickly.

GO 110 MILES IN 16 HOURS

And This Over A Trail Exceedingly Rough In Places—This Tribe Of Athletes Live In Mexico.

lived in Mexico, in the northern portion of the Mexican Sierra Madres.

In the early 1900s, American railroad contractors, who were building a mining railroad to the Tarahumara village of Bocoyna, were spellbound by the running exploits of the people who lived in the canyons. The workers amused themselves by wagering large sums of money on long-distance running races.

William Deming Hornaday

A historic 1906 race was held from Bocoyna to Minaca and back, about 110 miles on "exceedingly rough" trails over the mountains. **William Demming Hornaday** (1868-1942), an American journalist, and the publicity director for the National Railways of Mexico, was there to watch this race and reported that the Americans collected a purse of $100 for the winner.

"Great interest was manifested in the race, for the sum offered was quite a fortune to the members of the tribe. A council of war was immediately held by the chiefs, and two of the fastest runners were selected to do battle for the prize. The pair were also subjected to a close inspection by the Americans, who wagered large sums on the result."

On the day of this historic mountain trail ultramarathon, the two Tarahumara set off running through the rugged mountains. "The runners set out from Bocoyna first at a slow swinging gait. As they went along, they warmed to their work and the pace was quickened." The winner covered the 100+ mile course in 16 hours, looking fresh at the finish.

Consider that the 1906 Bocoyna-Minaca mountain trail 100-mile race predated Western States 100 by more than 70 years.

McEnery vs. Selby in California

Other isolated 100-mile races took place away from the Midwest. Two very rich men in California took up a bet to race against each other for more than 100 miles on rough dirt roads, railroad tracks, and trails.

At San Jose, California, on February 26, 1910, **Dr. William Augustine McEnery** (1873-1957) a former English distance running champion, married to a millionaire widow heir of Park City Utah silver mines, polo player, and globe trotter, raced against **Percy W. Selby** (1886-1969), a sturdy young real estate operator, heir of Selby smelting enterprise, golfer, and "a society man." The route chosen was thought to be about 108 miles between the Burlingame Country Club south of San Francisco to Hotel Del Monte in Monterey, California. Many wagers were made, more than $10,000 a week before the match.

"The match was brought about in this way: The doctor was chatting in the club the other day about the supreme devotion to sport of the English people. **Percy Selby** admitted that the English were great sporting people, but he remarked that of late years, the Americans seemed to get all the prizes when it came to international events. **Dr. McEnery** was a famous runner in Oxford and has many medals to show for his speed. Although not recently training, he offered to wager Selby $500 that he could defeat him in any long-distance kind of hike." The bet required that one of them finish in under 50 hours.

There was plenty of friendly trash-talking, leading up to the race. A story circulated that McEnery had paid Selby $200 to call the match off because his feet were sore from a short walk. But the next day, he was seen doing a 60-mile walk. "His talk of sore feet was all to lull Selby into a feeling of security so he would not train too hard."

Selby was well prepared, crewed by men in a one-horse carriage, with one famed walking trainer, **Phil Wand** (1869-1929), and a driver. He brought, "one-half dozen sponges, rubdown liniment, assorted shoes and sweaters, walking sticks, caps and hats, mineral waters and other liquids." McEnery's crew used an automobile, and his trainer was **Pat Kelly**.

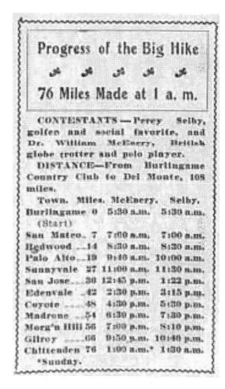

More than 1,000 automobiles containing friends of the two men were seen at the start at 5:30 a.m. The long procession followed along the way. "Both walkers were given a rub and while the morning was yet dark, the starting pistol broke the silence of the club grounds and McEnery and Selby were on their way. The onlookers cheered the men for over a mile down the road. Words of encouragement such as 'Get his cork, Percy,' 'Go after him Doc,' and 'Put an egg in your shoe and beat it' echoed for half an hour along the highway."

From the start they averaged about five m.p.h. "The two men chatted freely with each other and their trainers. Selby carried a can, while McEnery walked with his hand swinging freely by his side." At Redwood City, mile 14, McEnery made a spurt "and left Selby in the lurch," building a 20-minute lead by Palo Alto, mile 19. At Sunnyvale, long before it became Silicon Valley, Selby tried to take a shortcut by using railroad tracks but lost considerable time in his route on the railroad ties. Along the way, the two would take brief rests at hotels in the towns. The trainers provided Selby with a rubdown when he stopped at the La Molle House in San Jose.

McEnery reached 50 miles in about 12 hours, content with his four-mile lead. By mile 66 at Gilroy, in 16 hours, he still held a four-mile lead.

As Dr. McEnery approached the finish, the porches of Hotel Del Monte was crowded with cheering spectators. He won in about 36:45, 20 miles ahead of Selby.

Selby had developed extreme leg soreness and after a painful decent coming down San Juan Hill, and hearing that McEnerny had finished, he turned in at Salinas at about 7 p.m. with plans to finish at his leisure later the next day. After starting again at midnight, with his crew walking the remaining miles with him, he limped into the finish nine hours later for a finish of about 51:30.

Selby had the respect of San Francisco. "Mr. Selby lost like a gentleman and a scholar. He lost the race, but not our esteem."

Eleanor Sears

The California race was highly publicized. It brought out the woodwork many who wanted to challenge McEnerny or beat his time on the route.

Eleanor Sears (1881-1968) was a famous athlete and tennis champion from Boston, Massachusetts. She was known as a "bad girl" in athletics because at times she wore pants like men, shocked spectators by playing in rolled-up sleeves, crashing men-only squash courts, and broke through the Harvard Club's ban on women. She succeeded in 19 sports when it wasn't thought important for women to succeed.

On March 31, 1910, Sears attempted the 108-mile walk/run from Burlingame, to Monterey, California, on the rough dirt roads, railroad tracks, and trails. All went well until she reached Gilroy, mile 66, in 19:40, at night. Her crew following along in a primitive automobile had dwindled, as the men pacing her were getting tired and left. Her male chaperone, **Francis Carolan**, forced her to stop because it would not be proper "for a young woman to crawl across high trestles and climb lonely mountain trails without the protecting presence of a masculine escort."

It was disappointing because Sears was feeling well, with plenty of energy, but out-walked three men who were pacing her. "She had already proved herself physically superior to the men who had walked beside her."

The next morning, she ate a large breakfast in the hotel. "Dozens of curious persons took a sly peep at the young woman who had put her endurance powers to test and created a real sensation."

100 Miles in Wooden Shoes

In February 1899, **Julius Hayes**, a grocer's assistant, won a wager of 500 francs by walking the streets of Paris for 100 miles. "His feet were badly swollen this morning, and though they were bleeding and blistered, he finished the last mile and then fell exhausted."

100-Mile Walk for Health

In 1909 **Emil Deitz** (1842-1909), an aged resident of Williamsport, Pennsylvania, took a walk of over 100 miles "just for the fresh air." He disappeared from his home, leaving no trace of his whereabouts. He had sent a will to a friend, written in German on an old piece of a flour sack. His nephew, **William Parson Wallis** (1873-1931), searched all over the regions and finally found him aided by rural mailmen. "The old man, nearly exhausted after having subsisted solely on berries that grew by the wayside, was glad to return home." He died five months later.

Daniel O'Leary Walks 100 Miles and More

Daniel O'Leary

Pedestrian legend **Daniel O'Leary** of Chicago turned 80 in 1921. Despite his advanced age, he continued to walk and impress his audiences. On February 20, 1921, at age 79, he competed in a 200-mile race at the Main Street Auditorium in Houston, Texas, on a track 18 laps to the mile. He walked against **W. H. Guy** and **Charles Howe** (1894-1961), both of Houston. After eight hours, O'Leary reached 46 miles, only three miles behind the others. "Many admirers of the aged pedestrian visited the auditorium. While he was not in the lead throughout the day, they were confident that before the long grind had ended that he would be up there fighting for the lead. O'Leary's last walk of note was made in Cubs' Park at Chicago, when he stepped off 100 miles in 23:43."

O'Leary reached 100 miles in under 24 hours and continued on at a little better than four miles per hour pace. Guy led the race until the morning of the second day and quit because of blistered feet. "O'Leary had loaned him a specially built pair of walking shoes. Even then, the Houston man was noticed to limp." How also

O'LEARY IS NOW ONLY HIKER IN LONG PED RACE

Other Contestants With-draw After Hard Grind;

returned because of sore feet after reaching 98 miles. O'Leary continued on and reached at least 139 miles.

Zuni Races 100 Miles Against a Horse

During the 1920s, there was a lot of attention given to the impressive expertise of the American indigenous long-distance runners. But there was also some exploitation by others to use them in marketing and other

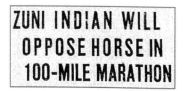

ZUNI INDIAN WILL OPPOSE HORSE IN 100-MILE MARATHON

activities for gain.

A Zuni from New Mexico, **Andrew Chimoni**, age 29, was particularly talented. It was claimed that in 1927 that he broke the world marathon record at Gallup, New Mexico. He was a finalist to compete at the 1928 Olympics in Amsterdam. On June 22, 1929, a 100-mile race was organized in Pecos, Texas, by **Mike Kirk**, featuring Chimoni racing against a thoroughbred west Texas distance horse.

Chimoni Ready to Race

"Chimoni set out this morning to beat his opponent, *General* and at the end of the first hour had covered ten miles to nine for the horse. The Indian maintained his pace for almost another ten miles but was forced to drop out on the nineteenth lap of the mile track with a strained muscle. He was treated for some time by two Indian trainers and finally reentered the race after the horse had covered 29 miles and was ten miles ahead of him. The injured leg, however, was too much of a handicap and the Zuni gave up the race at the end of the 20th mile. The horse then had covered 39 miles."

Folklore over the years changed the story. In one version, Chimoni, barefoot on the course, stepped on a cactus near the end of the race, which allowed the horse to win. In another version, the horse fainted just short of the finish line allowing Chimoni to win. A third version had the horse dropping dead.

Canadian 100-Miler

On September 7-8, 1929, a 100-mile race was held on the road from Three Rivers to Montreal, Quebec, Canada and

Valleyfield Runner Wins 100-Mile Race

back. **Joe Gagne**, of Valleyfield, Quebec, won by more than two hours over **Girard Labranche**, with a time of 16:50:00. Trophies were awarded. Gagne went on to play baseball and hockey in later years.

College Students

College students got into the 100-mile game during the 1930s. In 1933, six naïve but determined students from the University of Cambridge, in England, set out to walk 100 miles in 24 hours from Cambridge to London and back. Their motivation was to win $500 or

Both Losers

Cambridge Men Try To Walk 100 Miles To London in 24 Hours

lose $10. Four of them were clearly in over their heads and quit early. Two others did well. **R. A. Mason** developed bad blisters but managed to make it to mile 90 before quitting. **G. N. Wilson** went the furthest but gave up at mile 95, with only a few minutes remaining. In 1934, four other Cambridge students fared better and finished 100 miles in 24 hours, winning the 50-1 bet.

CHAPTER ELEVEN

Wartime 100-Milers

After decades of 100-mile races, matches and successful finishes in less than 24 hours before 1930, the Great Depression turned ultrarunners' attention to more important matters – surviving. Opportunities to earn a living as a professional runner dried up as public interest waned. Memories of past accomplishments and records faded. Occasionally the newspapers would pull out of their dusty archives a story about Edward Payson Weston's walking wonders, which was treated as "believe it or not" oddities, rather than something that others could accomplish.

But the spark of running or walking 100 miles on foot still smoldered during the next two decades despite the severe difficulties of the Depression and World War II. Isolated 100-mile accomplishments took place to remind the public what the human body could do, but all still considered 100 miles to be very far and out of reach for all but freakish athletes.

Gruber's "Softies"

During the World War II years, 100-mile races ceased, but some solo endurance efforts were sparked due to comments made by **Brigadier General Edmund L. "Snitz" Gruber** (1879-1941) who stated that American youth were "soft." Gruber was the author and composer of the song "The Caissons Go Rolling Along." In January 1941, speaking

Declares U. S. Youth "Soft," Urges Better School Training

General Gruber Deplores Rejection of One Out of Every 2 Draftees; Advises More Vocational Education

before a church's men's club in Kansas City, Missouri, he said, "Our men have been living too soft a life." He stated that the military draft had revealed an astonishing weakness in the physical, vocational, and moral qualities of youth. He claimed that one out of every two youths were rejected because of physical fitness. Gruber died five months later during a game of bridge at the age of 61.

Gruber's comments cause a bit of an uproar and debate across America. Newspaper commentary included, "We know of no way to prove the general is in error and of no way to prove that he is right." But young men across the country provided some anecdotal proof that Gruber was wrong.

A week before Gruber's brash statement, **Ted Morton**, age 19, a former high school track star from Kansas City, was being denied a job as a clearing house messenger because the company's president didn't think he had the physical stamina for the work. He stated, "The lad looked rundown to me." Miffed over this rejection and mad about General Gruber's comments, Morton started a crusade to prove his doubters wrong.

Ted Morton

Morton first ran 34 miles in 13:29 with a moving time of 7:30 as proof. A $10 wager also pushed him along. He ran in alternating hours, resting an hour in between. His inspiring accomplishment was performed on a 400-yard high school track. The day after he said, "I feel fine today. Got up and went to church too. I hope the general hears about this."

The general did hear about it. Gruber wrote a letter of congratulations to the youth stating that he hoped the performance "would inspire other young men to watch their health and keep themselves in good physical condition." Morton was soon hired by the army as a messenger for a commanding officer and made daily walks and runs of 8-15 miles to deliver messages.

Morton continued to prove Gruber wrong, even after his death. In July 1941, he organized a 50-mile race in Kansas City that included six former track stars. The race was billed as "an attempt to prove that American youth is adequately fit to defend their country." Representatives from the AAU even came to watch, along with thousands of spectators. A six-mile course was used in Swope Park and the young men were required to rest for fifteen minutes every two hours.

ALL SET FOR A 50-MILE SPRINT—

"The oldest contestant, **Milton Graham**, a 30-year-old truck driver, gave out at the end of eight miles, complaining a football knee was troubling him. As the sun climbed and the mileage passed 20 miles, there was little running going on. Ted Morton collapsed three times on his fourth 6-mile lap, but he recovered sufficiently from severe leg cramps to finish second, dropping out at the 44-mile point."

19 YEAR OLD POSTAL CLERK RUNS 50 MILES

Bill Breidenthal Goes to Church Services After Finishing Race in 10 Hours, 17 Minutes

Bill Breidenthal (1920-1994), a 19-year-old mail clerk for Southwestern Bell Telephone Company, won the 50-mile race with a time of 10:17. Breindenthal's crew, comprising two amateur boxers, gave him massages 25 times during the race. They only brought rubbing alcohol, sugar cubes, and salt tablets. Breindenthal went on to serve in the army air corps. He died while serving in the war two years later at the age of 22.

Bill Breidenthal

The notoriety Morton received for his running exploits continued to spur him on. In September 1941, he attempted to run 100 miles in less than

24 hours, going from Nevada, Missouri to Kansas City, Missouri. Physicians warned him that he should not plan to run the entire stretch at one time. He ran on US highway 71 with the help of pacer **Frank Grantello**. Morton's girlfriend, **Betty Grantello**, daughter of his pacer, rode along providing support from a car. His crew said he ran 6-10 miles at a stretch and then rested 10-15 minutes. Morton was successful and reached 100 miles in 23:54.

Wartime 100-milers

Courageous 100-mile efforts took place during the World War II years in many forms. For example, in 1940, **Daniel Olecnovich** (1885-1971) a famous horse jockey who rode at Belmont Park, walked 100 miles through Poland as the Germans invaded. He

successfully made it to Italy and intended to return to the United States and train horses at Peepskill, New York.

In 1941, **E. G. Barbette**, of Canada, was determined to sign up and serve in the war. He walked 100 miles in two nights and

Walks to Join Up

a day in order to arrive in time at a recruitment office. "He walked without stopping to sleep, eating from a meager lunch which he carried with him. All the time it was raining, and the going was tough." He had to ford waist-deep through an icy stream with a strong current. His determination paid off. He passed the examination and left dressed in a uniform.

A Dutch marine, **Bert**, who visited the USO Club at Camp Davis, North Carolina, told an interesting tale to those there. When the Germans closed the schools in Holland, the students went off to work on the outlying farms. Bert became a farmhand about 100 miles from his home city of Amsterdam. He said, "Two days after Christmas I was in the field, and looking up, saw my mother standing close by. Thinking I was dreaming, I rubbed my eyes to wipe away the tears. Then my mother spoke saying 'Merry Christmas, son.' It really was my mother. She had walked the 100 miles to be with me on Christmas, but the journey had taken her longer than she had anticipated, and so she was two days late."

Many 100-mile marches took place around the world. In 1942, many Australian troops completed a 100-mile march in the Middle East. They marched with full equipment and took five days. Also, in 1943, 4,000 soldiers marched 100 miles across the Blue Mountains from Sydney to Bathurst in Australia. One of the first Italian infantry units marched 100 miles that year through the Calabria Mountains to join the Allies.

Rangers in the United States Army received especially tough training. "Their training included toughening up day and night exercises in which they often marched 100 miles in two days with little rest and few rations. Such marches led them through rivers and up precipitous cliffs. They wiggled through barbed wire and dense undergrowth, and to simulate battle conditions, live bullets whizzed over head or kicked up dust behind them."

Lt. Omar N. Bradley (1893-1981), who at one time was overall commander of American troops fighting in France, earlier had served at Fort Riley, Kansas where his horse-drawn artillery battery was the first known unit to complete a 100-mile forced march in less than 24 hours! Yes, even in the army sub-24-hour 100-milers were accomplished by men in uniform.

In June 1943, the army conducted a forced march of 100 miles from Atlanta to Fort Benning, Georgia. The purpose was to assess the readiness of the 176th infantry soldiers for battle.

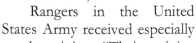

100-Mile March To Test Mettle Of U. S. Infantry

The men were picked at random, and they marched about 40 miles per day. The results helped determine what speed foot troops could cover over a distance of 100 miles "and still be able to put up a good fight at the conclusion of the march."

The Paratrooper 115-mile March

Colonel Robert Frederick Sink (1905-1965), commanding officer over the 506th US Parachute Infantry Regiment, in the 101st Airborne Division, wanted to conduct a "toughening practice" and felt his men could do better than the Japanese. The Regiment was located at a paratrooper training school at Fort Benning, in Georgia.

Robert Sink

Robert Sink graduated from West Point in 1927 and was commissioned as an Infantry Officer. In 1937, he served in the Philippines and then was stationed at Fort Huachuca in Arizona. As the war began, he was assigned to the 503rd Parachute Infantry Regiment and in July 1942 was named the commander of the 506th. During the war, he would turn down promotions in order to stay with his unit. He would be at both D-day and the Battle of the Bulge.

The Parachute School

Paratroopers spent thirteen weeks at the school for basic training at Fort Benning, Georgia. Trainees were selected from other basic training units to become paratroopers and went through four weeks of jump training. This consisted of many hours of tumbling exercises, learning to somersault safely to their feet. They also learned how to twist their parachute lines in descent to always land with their back to the wind. To become accustomed to the shock of a parachute opening, they would jump from a 20-foot-high platform, wearing parachute harness attached to a steel cable. They would also

make descents in a standard size parachute from a 250-foot tower. All this finally prepared them for five leaps from an airplane, qualifying them as a full-fledged paratrooper.

Toccoa to Atlanta

Colonel Sink organized a three-day march from Camp Toccoa to Atlanta, Georgia, about 115 miles. Both officers and NCOs had to complete the entire distance or risk being thrown out of the unit. **Colonel G. H. Williams**, the assistant commandant at the parachute school, explained the reasoning for this march. "What we learned of the operation of our men in Africa convinced us of the soundness of our program of hard muscle building and strict discipline. One of the units in the invasion marched 30 miles after getting on the ground and then captured the airport which was their objective."

On December 4, 1942, Sink and 600 paratroopers set off to achieve their goal. Each man carried full combat equipment, including mortars, machine guns, and other arms. **Major Robert Lee Wolverton** (1814-1844), "a husky West Pointer," set the pace. They marched in fog, rain, sleet and hail, through soggy fields and along concrete highways. On one night, they camped on the banks of a lake on the Oglethorpe University campus. Buses were kindly rushed out to transport the Paratroopers to a country club for hot showers.

During the long days, some fell out for a time to nurse sore feet but caught up. They refused rides offered by passing motorists. Sink congratulated those who fell out, "When you fell, you fell face forward."

Private **Leonard Hicks** recalled he had the toughest job in the whole outfit. It was his duty to run, not walk, ahead of the battalion to set up roadblocks on the side roads so traffic wouldn't hinder the marching men. As the last man would pass him, Hicks would wave the cars on and again run ahead to set up the next roadblocks. He was the first to arrive in Atlanta and thus the first to get a hot bath. His feet were very sore, and his boots were caked with red mud from the Georgia back roads.

Once they all arrived, the mayor of Atlanta presented each of them with a ribbon from the city of Atlanta. The soldier's moving time over the 115 miles was 31 hours. They claimed it was a new world's forced march record. Col. Sink said the march was "unparalleled in continental American history."

The paratroopers arrive in Atlanta

Robert Wolverton

From Atlanta, the soldiers were transported to Fort Benning, except for one battalion. Instead of getting a ride, the battalion, led by Major Wolverton, marched on to Fort Benning after only a couple of days' rest. During this extended march, Wolverton's feet became so swollen that he couldn't wear his boots. He marched a portion of the of the time wearing only three or four pairs of socks. They covered 136 miles in four days, but with less moving time than the march to Atlanta. They proclaimed they bettered the world record for forced marching. As they arrived at Fort Benning, they were "singing, cursing, and nursing sore feet." **Robert Wolverton** died in 1944 on D-day at Normandy.

100 miles across the Sahara Desert

In 1943, **Sergeant Alban Petchal** (1920-1977), of Steubenville, Ohio, was on a plane flying as a gunner, heading to the war in Africa. When they reached Central Africa, near a combat zone, Petchal's plane became separated from the rest and wound up running out of gas over the Sahara Desert. "They rode the plane into the sand dunes, which were everywhere,

160

and about two stories high. They bounced across the tops of four and slammed head on into the fifth. All three men were painfully hurt."

The men crawled out of the wrecked plane, patched up their wounds and made a shelter out of their life raft. After three days, the three wounded men decided that they would have to walk out of the desert. They sprinkled the plane with gasoline and set it on fire. They then started off on what they knew would be a perilous 100-mile journey carrying a five-gallon can of water slung from a stick. Along the way, they battled sickness and freezing nights. Two officers became delirious and quarreled violently. "Finally, they found tracks, and the same day ran onto a camel caravan. The Arabs fed them and allowed them to join them. The boys tried to ride the camels, but it was so rough and horrible that they finally had to get off and walked." After walking a total of 100 miles across the desert, they finally arrived at a French unit.

Prisoners of War 100-mile marches

As prisoners were captured during the war, once freed, many told tales of 100-mile marches as prisoners of war. The most famous, and probably the most tragic, was the "Death March of Bataan" in the Philippines. The distance was likely quite a bit less than 100 miles, but to those who participated and survived, it typically was described as a 100-mile journey.

After four months of intense battle, on April 9, 1942, American troops surrendered to the Japanese. The captured Americans and Filipinos were subjected to a torturous march of more than 65 miles, during which thousands died. Many books have been written about the event.

Lt. James Kermit Vann (1924-1976) described his "100-mile death march." He felt lucky that he survived the march, but he suffered terribly. He wrote, "This prisoner army of almost 3,000, most of them dirty, ragged and unshaven was led to a road and

under cloudless skies was ordered to march. None of us got any water until nightfall. We had passed many natural wells off the road, but the bayonets wouldn't let us near them."

"At times we were ordered to sit down in the road under the hot sun. Anyone who tried to stand up was knocked down. Anyone who tried to stretch out his legs was forbidden to relax. We sat there for four or five hours. It wasn't long before I

came down with malaria, beriberi, dysentery, and other ailments. It wasn't until the fifth day that we were given any food. There was almost no conversation among the men. They were too sick, too weak, too hollow-eyed and sunken-cheeked to care about anything except home. I was so weak and dizzy that I don't remember too much about the rest of the march. I believe we made the 100-mile march in seven days." 100-mile runners are concerned about losing too much weight during their events. Lt. Vann lost 55 pounds during his march, to a weight of 105 pounds.

There were also prisoner 100-mile marches to Germany. **Lt. Donald Alfred Ohl** (1920-2011) of Iowa City, Iowa was crossing the Moselle in France with his unit in September 1944. "The bridge we crossed was blown up behind us. I found myself looking down the mouth of a German 88-

millimeter cannon." The men were marched 100 miles to the German border, with 45 miles of it in one day. Lt. Ohl suffered from broken arches in his feet. After the second day's march they were handed over to the SS, put into prison cells, and eventually sent off to a Stalag. At the end of the war, he was freed.

100 miles to Germany

In 1944, near the end of the war in Europe, the German army was in retreat from France. Thousands of Allied prisoners were being held at Montigny, France. They were told by their German captors that they were going to be marched 100 miles through the war chaos to Germany. **John Mecklin** (1918-1971) was an American correspondent who had been taken prisoner and wrote about the terrifying 100-mile march. About 2-3,000 men began the 100-miler in a column about a mile long.

John Mecklin

"When we started, we were in reasonably good spirits, but that did not last long. After an hour or two, the whole column moved in sullen, beaten silence." The men and the Germans were in constant fear of being bombed by American planes who had no idea that a prisoner 100-mile march was taking place. "We made an ideal air target. The road ran almost entirely through open, rolling fields. Even the ditches were too shallow for good protection. I carried a blanket, a musette bag, a canteen of water, toilet articles and two cans of German tinned meat, and with each step the load became heavier."

The Germans set the initial pace, but before long, the prisoners, who were younger and in better shape, took over the pace. Finally, the exhausted Germans decided to use a bus to shuttle prisoners in a round-robin fashion up the road in five-mile stretches. Cheating the 100-mile course for stretches was a luxury as they rode with their guard in a corner of the bus with a revolver balanced in his lap.

At Bourbonne-les-Bains, the 100-miler became a pure "endurance contest." They walked steadily for three hours without rest. The Germans knew they were racing ahead of the advancing Allied forces and were very nervous. Finally, the bus crashed into a ditch and was broken down. There would be no more rides during this 100-miler. When a small pickup truck came by, the Germans elbowed each other to pile in, one sobbing that he could walk no farther. But the Americans had no choice but to continue their long walk.

"The whole atmosphere among the men in the column was beginning to change. They became a sweaty, dragging anguish. Panic was beginning to seep into the minds of the men on that endless road, while the sun beat down and seared everything. When the column passed villages, we prisoners would straighten up and walk firmly."

As they continued on, the Germans started talking in low voices and the prisoners feared that they would soon be shot. A guard told them that they could run into the woods and escape around the next bend. Was he trying to give them a reason to get shot? Mecklin and a few others went off the 100-mile course and dashed into the woods. They threw away all that they carried and ran at top speed and then tried to find someone to put them up for the night. Finally, at dusk, three men came toward them and to their relief, they wanted to help. "They took us to an ancient mill on the edge of the village and, before long, we were the center of attraction at a full-dress banquet. Fifty people came to visit us within an hour. We went out with the people to stand in the square and sing the French national anthem. An officer said, 'You are free. The Germans will not be back.'" It was one of the greatest celebrations for DNFing a 100-miler in history.

Korean War 100-mile Marches

During the Korean War, 100-mile death marches took place. In July 1950, **Burdett Wayne Eggen** (1932-1974), age 18 from North Hollywood, California, experienced his first and only day of combat. He was with 1,800 men who were told to take three hills but were ambushed near Hadong. Only 125 survived, including Eggen, who played dead but discovered and captured.

After being held in a church that then was bombed and strafed, the surviving prisoners were taken to a prisoner of war camp in Seoul. But after a month, Eggen and others were forced to march 100 miles to

Pyongyang to stay ahead of advancing US troops. Eggen said, "During the march they fed us things like dog biscuits. We didn't have much water, but the biscuits had to be soaked before you could eat them. But pretty soon even the biscuits ran out, and we had nothing to eat except what we could steal along the way."

They were divided up into groups of 50 and those in the last group, the weakest, would get shot when they fell out. "Everybody tried to help his buddies, half carrying the weaker ones along." At the finish of their 100-miler, they were taken further by train and stopped near a tunnel. Most of Eggen's group of 30 were massacred there, and he was shot in the leg and again played dead. Six survived, went into the woods and later were found and rescued by American airborne troops.

CHAPTER ELEVEN

Wally Hayward

100-mile attempts mostly ceased across the world during the 1940s because of World War II. By 1946 some isolated 100-mile attempts reemerged, including a walking event in England where seven athletes accomplished the distance in less than 24 hours. **Rex Whitlock** of Great Britain walked the 100-mile Bath Road course in an amazing 17:44:40 in 1952.

Ultrarunning, at other distances, also came to life again in South Africa when the Comrades Marathon (55 miles) was held again in 1946 and the Pieter Korkie 50 km was established in Germiston. In England, the London to Brighton running race (52 miles) was established in 1951, using the famed road that was used by walking and biking events decades earlier. Ultrarunning was reawakening.

Hundreds of runners attempted and completed 100-mile events during the prewar decades. Would the 100-miler truly come back in the modern era of ultrarunning?

World War II formally concluded, but conflicts continued across the world. During the aftermath of the war, with evolving superpowers, the changing world map, and the resulting Cold War, it made it a difficult time for ultrarunning to emerge widely. But the running sport has always been resilient.

Wally Hayward

South Africa continued to take the lead in producing the greatest 100-mile runners of the time. **Wallace "Wally" Henry Hayward** (1908-2006) was another elite runner following the running steps of **Arthur Newman** and **Hardy Ballington**. Hayward would become one of the greatest 100-mile runners ever. His father died when Wally was young and, at age sixteen, he started working as an apprentice carpenter in South Africa.

A friend talked Hayward into taking a running job, to put in stakes for diamond mining claims. Hayward said, "I had never run before, but he said I would be fine as I was always running and walking everywhere." They would represent prospectors and run to stake in square claims with pegs.

One huge claim run involved about 6,000 runners from age 8 to 70. Prospectors gave the runners an idea where they wanted their claims and when the flag dropped for the start, it was a mass stampede to go stake the best claims.

Hayward described the chaos. "When I got to the spot that I was to peg, there was an argument going on between a man who pegged some valuable claims and two big bullies who pulled his pegs out and put their own in. There was a big dispute which resulted in the poor man who pegged first being beaten up and his leg broken."

Formal Running Begins

In 1927, at the age of 19, he joined a Boy's Club and was invited to go running. His first run ended up being for 10 miles, which he thought was nuts. He said, "In those days, there was no one to tell you how or when you should run. There were no books to advise you. I used to go out training every afternoon." He ran in a few races and at the end of 1929, read about the Comrades Marathon. He wrote to the race director **Vic Clapham**, and was shocked in the reply to learn that the race was about 54-56 miles. His longest run up to that point was 37 miles. He decided to enter the 1930 race.

Hayward was clearly a rookie at the 1930 Comrades and went out fast. By the halfway point, he surprised everyone and held a 29-minute lead. Clapham warned him that if he didn't ease up, he would hit the wall, and he did, going up Polly Shorts. But he generally held it together enough to win by 31 seconds with a time of 7:27:26. He would go on to win Comrades five times.

In 1931, Hayward broke a bone in his foot while training for Comrades and the next year was told by a doctor that some chest pains he was feeling was because of a strained heart. At age 23, he was told to never run again. He put running aside for a few years until a specialist told him the diagnosis was "rubbish" and told him to go home and put on his running shoes. By 1938, he was competing again.

Hayward would run many miles alone on the trails. He wrote, "Sometimes I would run anything from two to six hours cross-country just for the pleasure it gave me, jumping over bushes, running through forests and swamp lands, traversing rivers, anything for fun. By the time I reached home, I am sure many people used to say to themselves, 'There's a scruffy and dirty looking guy. I wonder if he ever has a bath or washes his clothes.'"

With the outbreak of World War II, Hayward was assigned to the South African Engineer Corp. working in railroad construction, building and fixing bridges. As he became stationed in Egypt, he was known to run at least five miles before breakfast. He also ran while in Italy and Syria.

Post-war Running

Hayward returned from the war in 1945, worked as a building inspector, and started training seriously. He would often run home from work, returning after dark at 10 p.m. After being away from Comrades for 20 years, he ran again in 1950 and won. The next year, 1951, he broke the "down record" in 6:14:08. That year, he was recognized as being the top amateur athlete in Africa and was chosen to run on the 1952 Olympic marathon team. He finished tenth in the Helsinki games.

Hayward said that 1953, at age 45, was his greatest running year. First, he won Comrades in an astonishing record time of 5:52:30, the first to break six hours. Next, he went to England to compete on the world stage. He got four-months' leave from his job and mortgaged his home to raise money for expenses. He first went and ran the London to Brighton *running* race, formally in its third year. He boarded with **Arthur Newton**, who passed on valuable advice. The British running community was very curious about how he would do, knowing that he was unbeaten in ultra-distances.

It was clear shortly after the start that Hayward was out to win. Soon after 20 miles, he went into the lead and was ahead of the course record pace set by

S. AFRICAN ATHLETE SETS UP NEW RECORD
W. Hayward Runs Away with London-Brighton Road Race

Newton. At Crawley, he couldn't use the railway level crossing because of a train, so he ran down the steps into the subway beneath the line. By 40 miles, he was well ahead of the field and went on to win in 5:29:40, breaking the course record time by 22 minutes. His time also beat the unofficial world 50-mile road record by three minutes held by Hardy Ballington.

100-mile World Record

It finally was time for Hayward to attempt to run 100 miles. He planned to try to break **Hardy Ballington's** world best time of 13:21:19 on Bath Road, from Box to London. **Derek Ernest Reynolds** (1914-1962) age, 39, of England and 20-year-old **Jackie Mekler** (1932-2019) of South Africa also took part in this "time trial" that took place on October 4, 1953. Newton gave advice to the rookie 100-mile runners

Hayward, Reynolds, and Mekler at the start

about "hitting the wall" at about mile 70. Running legend, **Peter Gustav Gavuzzi** (1905-1981) was Hayward's crew chief that day.

Gavuzzi suggested the runners receive enemas before going to bed the evening before in order to save time spent in the bushes during the race. They went to bed early for the early morning start.

Mekler wrote, "This was exciting stuff for the local inhabitants, many of whom stayed on in the bar at the hotel until the start of the race. A lively party was still going strong when we arrived for a light breakfast at 2:30 a.m. It was absolutely bizarre eating this early morning meal amidst the blaring music being thumped out of a piano. The party came to an abrupt end when we were called to the start. Apart from a pool of light from the hotel, it was pitch dark." They were off and running at 3 a.m.

Hayward wrote, "I set off with a good measure of confidence and ran steadily for the whole race." At 25 miles, he was 10 minutes behind record time,

SOUTH AFRICAN SETS 100-MILE RUN RECORD

but by 50 miles, he was 16 minutes ahead. He added, "Fortunately, I didn't hit the wall as Newton predicted, for which I was thankful. My time was 12:20:28. I broke Ballington's record by 1 hour, 53 minutes." It was reported, "The South African finished with a sprint and was given a great ovation by the waiting crowd as he broke tape. His nearest rivals were more than an hour behind him." It was believed to be a world record at the time, although the Bath Road course was never certified and thought to be quite a bit short of 100 miles.

24 hours World Record

With the 100-mile world record achieved, **Arthur Newton** encouraged Hayward to go after the 24-hour world record. Hayward wrote, "I was somewhat dumbfounded, bearing in mind 72 miles was my longest ever training run. 100 miles was bad enough. Now he wanted me to tackle a world record that stood at over 152 miles. The man was nuts."

The attempt was arranged at very short notice for judges, timekeepers, lap scorers, and others. The venue selected was Motspur Park in Surrey. The University of London built the Motspur Park athletics stadium in 1928 and it achieved fame when the world mile record was set there in 1938. In 1952, **Derek Reynolds** ran a world record 50 miles on this track in 5:30:22, so it was a fast cinder 440-yard track surface.

Hayward was still suffering some leg pain from the 100-miler but was reasonably confident that he could compete well. Six runners competed, with his main competition coming from **Derek Reynolds** of the Blackheath Harriers, winner of London to Brighton in 1952, and the 50-mile world record holder.

Newton and Gavuzzi again assisted Hayward with pre-race preparation and race strategy. "They based Hayward's schedule on the theory that one had to put in a lot of miles early on to make up for the final hours, when the pace was sure to drop." They believed he could reach 170 miles.

The historic race began on November 20, 1953, at 11 a.m. in foggy weather. Hayward started out running comfortable seven-minute

Newton assists Hayward

miles. He reached 50 miles in 6:06:34 with a 12-minute lead. "By 60 miles I was ahead of the existing world record for the intermediate distances and broke the 100-mile track world record with a time of 12:46:34, the first to break 13 hours."

After reaching 100 miles, he came off the track for his only long stop for a massage and a bowl of rice pudding. After a half-hour rest, cramping set in and he could hardly walk. A veteran marathoner observed, "I think Wally made a big mistake when he came off the track. I remember him being laid out on the massage table in the changing rooms. He had stiffened up so much that it was as if rigor mortis had set in. We took it in turns trying to massage some life back into his legs. His huge calf muscles were solid, like oak."

Eventually, he managed to jog on in a painful, awkward-looking style. At dawn he was moving with about ten-minute-miles, with four more hours to go. Reynolds was catching up, and this helped motivate Hayward to push on.

Newton, age 70, and Gavuzzi kept him well-supplied with tea, soup, and custard. "all the hot drinks were prepared on a little stove. In the early hours, I threw a major tantrum because my drinks were not hot, only to be told they had just come off the stove."

World Record Set In 24-Hour 'Sprint'

At 22:41:21, Hayward broke Newton's 152-mile 24-hour world record set in 1931, but in the last 80 minutes could only manage five miles an hour. He finished with 159 miles, 562 yards, a new 24-hour world record. Reynolds finished in second place, reaching 100 miles 13:35:27, and finishing with 154 miles in 24 hours. Hayward held the 24-hour world record for the next 20 years.

Hayward wasn't terribly pleased with this performance. He said the veins in the right calf of his leg gave him severe pains during the last ten hours. At the finish he said, "Thank God that's over. Never again, it was awful." It was reported, "He flopped exhausted on a dressing room bench and scarcely seemed interested as aides told him he had smashed

every known record from eight hours up. During the monotonous jogging around the oval track he lost seven pounds." He ate two pounds of sugar, drank a pint of tomato soup, and a pint of milk, in which were six beaten eggs.

Later he reflected, "I really made a hash of it. Coming off that track at 100 miles was the biggest mistake I ever made. I just couldn't get going again. For me, it was a wasted opportunity. I should have gone considerably further than I did. If anyone breaks my record, good luck to them."

It was reported in England, "Records fell like autumn leaves and even the officials lost count of the number which Hayward broke, but all the known world figures from eight hours and 64 miles,

6 search results		
Rank	Performance	Surname, first name
1	256.399 km	Hayward, Wallace H. (Wally)
2	248.960 km	Reynolds, Derek E.
3	193.348 km	Griffiths, Leslie H.
4	141.622 km	Legge, John C.
5	99.376 km	Jones, Stan
6	80.467 km	Perkin, Fred H.

most of which were established in the 1880s both in England and America were bettered by Hayward."

About the general experience, he said, "This type of race eventually gets very boring. Like a pig with its snout to the ground, you circulate, lap after lap after lap." At the airport to fly back to South Africa, Hayward said, "After the run I said I was finished, but fools always try these things again."

After a few months, he was ready to compete again. His trip to England cost £550, worth $20,500 in 2020.

1954 100-mile attempt

On July 17, 1954, at the age of 46, Hayward made another attempt to break the 100-mile world record, this time on a road in South Africa from Standerton to Germiston in mid-winter. The weather turned bad with a strong wind a few hours before the start. Hayward ate a pre-race meal of a huge steak, two eggs, and 12 slices of brown bread and jam. He was away running at 1 a.m. and said, "It was so bitter cold that I put my tracksuit top on, which was not much use, as first the rain began, followed by sleet. On top of this, I was running into a 40-mph headwind. The judges suggested I abort the run and try in better conditions, but I refused. I was determined to carry on, come what may."

His crew chief, **Fred Morrison**, kept him full of hot tea or coffee and would throw a heavy woolen blanket over his head and shoulders during his stops. Despite the challenging conditions, he made good progress and in the morning was joined by boys from a local orphanage. He reached 50 miles in 6:20:35.

With just a few miles to go in the afternoon, he still had hopes of breaking the record. However, a steep hill took its toll on him. "Hundreds of people, including my wife and daughter, congregated at Germiston Lake to welcome me at the finish. The crowd gave me a great cheer as I completed the final mile lap and breasted the tape in 13:08:08. This was a new South African record, but well outside my world record time of 12:20:28."

A local reporter wrote, "He missed the world record for the simple reason that he had mistimed, not his run, but the season. He should have tried in summer. At one time, the temperature was below zero C."

Hayward's amateur career came to end later that year when the South Africa Amateur and Cycling Association declared him as a professional, claiming he broke rules for accepting funds directly from donors for his record attempts in England. The declaration was highly controversial and condemned throughout the

country. He said, "The whole episode was very, very distressing. It was grossly unfair and left me a bitter man. I had done my best for South Africa, and this had to happen." His 100-mile running career came to an end.

The ban from competition remained until 1974. At 70 in 1978, he finished a marathon in an impressive 3:06:24. In 1988, at the age of 79, he finished Comrades in under 10 hours, beating half of the field. He finished again the next year at the age of 80. It was reported, "Shortly before the start, Hayward, a few weeks short of his 81st birthday, fell awkwardly as he stepped off a pavement in Pietermaritzburg. Many of us have witnessed the consequences of a fall for an octogenarian. Often, it is what concerned family members tend to call 'the beginning of the end.' Hayward's response was somewhat different. He got up, dusted himself off and proceeded to complete the Comrades Marathon. It wasn't his most impressive run. He only just beat the time limit and was hospitalized for a few days. But he made it!"

Wally Hayward passed away at the age of 97 in 2006.

CHAPTER TWELVE

Various 100 Mile Attempts 1950-1960

Frank Tozer – Prolific 100-mile Walker

Frank Wallace Tozer was born May 24, 1879, in South Bristol, New York. He became a farmer from Ithaca, New York and in 1910, at the age of 31, stirred up attention when he departed on a long endurance walk to New Orleans, Louisiana. He claimed he was accustomed to walking long distances and his hobby was pedestrianism. He delivered lectures along the way.

He also became a bicycle enthusiast and in 1926 pedaled all the way to Florida. Tozer gained wide fame in 1938, when he set out from Ithaca, New York, accompanying two others, a policeman, and

Frank Tozer

a fireman, on a 34-mile walking race to Elmira, New York. Tozer finished first in 7:50, beating the policeman, **Daniel B. Flynn** (1893-1959) by nearly three hours. After arriving, Tozer declined a ride home and completed his return trip in 8:20.

ATTEMPTS TO WALK HERE AND BACK TO ITHACA IN 24 HOURS

Tozer Tired and Dusty, but Confident He'll Achieve His Goal

Tozer quickly added to this accomplishment in August 1938 by attempting a 100-mile walk to Binghamton, New York, and back in 24 hours. He previously had accomplished it in 26 hours. He said, "Only a rainstorm will stop me." It was reported at the 50-mile mark in Binghamton, "He was tired and dusty, but undaunted. Frank Tozer walked into the offices of the *Binghamton Press* after 12 ½ hours. He was confident that he would be able to return to Ithaca before the deadline."

But the 59-year-old walker had difficulty on his return trip. He tried to take a shorter route but made a wrong turn and walked bonus miles. When the 24 hours expired, he was still about 20 miles from the finish. He learned that he really needed to have a crew car drive along with him. He stated, "When you are walking against time, you don't have any time to stop and make inquiries. I would have been better off with help like that."

In 1943, Tozer, age 64, was living in **Man Takes 100-Mile Walk For Vacation** Harrisburg, Pennsylvania, and wanted to prove that war travel restrictions couldn't prevent people from getting away on vacations if they really wanted to go. He planned a 100-mile course that involved a road walk from Harrisburg to York and back for the first 55 miles, a five-mile walk through Harrisburg, and for the last 40 miles, forty crossings of a mile-long bridge across the Susquehanna River. He was successful in accomplishing the 100 miles in 24 hours on Memorial Day.

Tozer returned to Ithaca in 1943 and was employed at the Cornell University Library. In November 1945, at the age of 66, he measured off a two-mile stretch and walked it repeatedly to reach 100 miles during a 24-hour period. This walk was very challenging because of a bitter cold wind. He was paced by **Orhan Illgaz,** a college student from Turkey who usually walked 6-7 miles per day. For 1946, Tozer walked around Cayuga Lake and through several towns to accomplish 100 miles again.

At age 68, in 1947, Tozer explained his secret to a long, happy life. "Eat right, sleep right and walk 10 miles a day." Each day, as weather permitted, he walked to and from work for a round trip of 10 miles. He would encourage young people to walk with him, but they would give up trying to match his pace. He added that each summer he tried to get in at least one 100-mile 24-hour walk. "He has been taking these 'century walks' for his pleasure and health chiefly to test his stamina and to determine for himself that he could still take it."

During May 1947, he attempted to walk 100 miles from Ithaca to Rochester, New York to deliver a letter to the newspaper there and to visit relatives. His first attempt was a bust because of a bad rainstorm along the way, that caused bad blisters. But in July he was successful and finished his 100 miles in less than 24 hours, perhaps the first American to accomplish a sub-24-hour 100-miler in the modern, post-war era of ultrarunning.

On January 11, 1950, at the age of 70, Tozer died of a stroke while in the Cornell University Library. "Fellow workers found the famed long distance walking man in the steam room of the institution."

Mote Bergman

Alvin Floyd "Mote" Bergman (1887-1978) of Leetsdale, Pennsylvania was a professional pre-war ultrarunner who competed regularly in a 50-mile "Pittsburgh Leader Race," in the years around 1915. That year, at the age of 28, he achieved his most proud accomplishment. He walked from Pittsburgh to Chicago, a distance of about 503 miles in seven days. During that trip, he walked with pedestrian legends, **Daniel O'Leary** of Chicago and **Edward Payson Weston** of New York.

In 1931, Mote "hiked" from New York to Pittsburgh in seven days and stated that "he thinks nothing of walking 50 miles a day." For a couple of days, he covered 67 miles in 15-16 hours each day. He said, "Everybody ought to forget their autos for an hour a day and walk five or six miles. It's the greatest health builder in the world."

His local fame increased. He was mentioned in *Ripley's Believe it or Not* publication. In 1936 he accomplished a 55-mile walk to Sharon, Pennsylvania, fueled only by a saucer of grapefruit at the start. When he arrived, the mayor and a band greeted him. In 1937, at age 50, his birthday walks began to get attention nationally. He said, "A man is as old as his legs."

Walking 100 miles in a day became Bergman's goal. In 1939, at age 52, he took his walking talents to the Leetsdale High School track where he walked/ran 100 miles in 22:05 on the quarter-mile track. He would accomplish several other sub-24-hour 100s in the future. It was reported, "He frequently walks 20 miles before breakfast just to get up an appetite, and he always fasts as part of his training before a long-distance stroll."

In 1943, during the war, Mote was an auxiliary military police officer at a war plant. Gas rationing was in effect and the local newspaper thought it would be funny to do a feature on Mote because gas rationing was not a problem for Mote. It was reported, "Never in his life did he own an automobile. His only possible concern could be over his supply of walking shoes. But Mr. Bergman possesses five pairs, which at 5,000 miles to the pair and 500 miles to the sole, should last him for the duration." Whenever he would buy a new pair of shoes, he would put them on and wade in a bathtub full of water for an hour. Then he would go walk 40-50 miles, letting them dry on the way. He said, "The shoes squish around a little but walking around in them for the rest of the day takes care of the squish. They dry out and fit like gloves." The most miles he achieved in a pair of shoes was 10,000 miles. He would put a bit of tape around the backs of his shoes "to keep the stones from jumping in," an early version of gaiters.

On August 26, 1950, Bergman accomplished another sub-24-hour 100-mile walk. He walked through several towns with a car following to measure the distance on the odometer. When it showed 50 miles, he turned around and started back. He finished in about 23:30.

Mote continued his annual birthday walks and at age 65 walked from Detroit to Pontiac, Michigan and back, for the Detroit Elks Club. His wife, **Verna Bergman**, was asked about his walking hobby. She replied, "It's a better hobby than hunting or fishing. The only trouble is, he's always too tired to enjoy his own birthday parties."

Mote's most historic 100-mile run came in 1961 when he was 74 years old. The course was to walk between Leetsdale and Aliquippa, Pennsylvania, walking back and forth between the towns, along the Ohio River 8 ½ times. Two others entered to attempt

At 74, Mote Takes Another 100-Mile Walk

A. F. (Mote) Bergman, center, walks determinedly on Constitution Boulevard between Ambridge and Aliquippa. With him are John Oros, left, and Jack Hiller.

it, **John J. Oros** (1913-2001) and **Jack Lewis Hiller** (1930-2016), but once some storms arrived, they both dropped out. Mote reached 100 miles in 23:50, which was at least the 4th time he had walked 100 miles in less than a day. At the finish he was exhausted, but the only ill effect was a big blister on his left toe.

To recognize his 80th birthday, Mote made three round trips to West Aliquippa, Pennsylvania for 60 miles and then next day walked 20 miles to Oakland, Pennsylvania to celebrate with **Stan Musial** before a baseball game between the Pittsburgh Pirates and the St. Louis Cardinals. He still had never owned a car and said, "If I don't walk, I don't feel good."

In 1978, **Alvin F. "Mote" Bergman** died at the age of 90 in the Elks National Home, Bedford Virginia, where he had been living for the previous two years. He finished his walking career with about 385,000 miles. Mote set his mark on ultrarunning history by being one of the very few Americans who spanned the pre-war era of ultrarunning into the modern era. While he didn't take part in races after about 1948 because they were few, he most likely was the one of the first Americans to cover 100 miles in less than 24 hours during the modern era with his walks in 1950 and 1961.

Great Escape 100-miler

Boys Caught

100-Mile Trek From Monroe Proves Futile

In 1950, at Monroe, Louisiana, two boys aged 15 and 16, escaped from the Louisiana Training Institute and walked 100 miles in two days to Shreveport on railroad tracks. The police found both boys at the home of one of their mothers and took them into custody. "State troopers investigating the case said the boys had blisters as big as your fist on both feet."

Cotton Picker 100

During November 1951, about 100 migrant Mexican workers quit their cotton-picking jobs in west Tennessee and started a 100-miler. The men had been brought from Mexico to work on a plantation owned by **Terry Jamison**. He said they just "walked out" of their contract. The Mexicans had quit their job because of bad food and pay.

Cotton Pickers Walk Out

49 Mexicans in Memphis After 100-Mile Hike

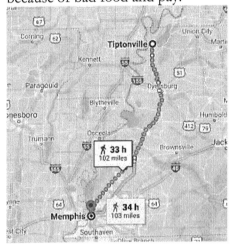

As of November 22, 1951, forty-nine of them had finished the 100 miles, arriving in Memphis, Tennessee, footsore and frightened, complaining bitterly about their working conditions to **Angel Cano**, the Mexican consul. The feet of most of the finishers were badly blistered. They were given government-paid lodging and food in a local hotel. Fifty-one other men were still on the road walking. Others were thrown in jail when they attempted to leave Tiptonville, Tennessee. A Sheriff admitted jailing about 20 of the 100-miler entrants. The group was eventually provided transportation back to their homeland.

Paul Smith – Oregon's Walking Man

Solo 100-mile attempts that were used to get public recognition and possible financial gain emerged again. **Paul Arthur Smith** (1884-1962) of Mill City Oregon was known locally as Oregon's "walking man" known before and after the war. In 1911, at the age of 26, he claimed he ran a very unlikely 130 miles from Bend to Burns, Oregon in 22:11:00. In 1926, when ultra-distance walking and running was still popular, Smith walked/ran 100 miles from Salem to Portland and back in a best-known time of 16:26:10. (The distance probably was closer to 90 miles). His true fame came in 1928. Smith finished 21st in **C. C. Pyle's** race across America (The Bunion Derby).

After the war, in 1949, Smith still hoped to be a professional ultrarunner. He gained national fame when he raced a horse for 75 miles on a half-mile oval track. The horse won by 14 miles.

In 1951, Smith was 66 years old, and he announced he would try to break his own 100-mile "record," this time walking from Bend, Oregon to Mill City, Oregon. The route involved a net descent of about 3,000 feet. Smith was a former miner, tall and weighed 190 pounds. He said he had trained for the event by walking a couple hundred miles. The Mill City Chamber of Commerce sponsored his attempt and attached it to a big aviation day celebration.

Smith began his 100-miler. Walking during the night brought some excitement. Smith said, "Some fellow in a car apparently didn't see me and zoomed by so close that the sandwich I was about to eat flew out of my hand and was lost. And later on, I thought I heard somebody walking behind me. When I looked back a few times, I saw nothing, but still heard steps that weren't mine. Then suddenly something nipped at my heel and when I kicked at it, I found that the thing was a porcupine. He ran away into the woods when I kicked at him, and lucky for me, I missed him."

Walking for so long at about 4,000 feet altitude, dried up Smith's mouth. He tried to spit but instead, out came his false teeth. He said, "I was lucky again. Just as I spit 'em out, I made a grab and caught 'em before they hit the pavement."

Smith finished his 100-miler in 17:06:06, missing his record by 40 minutes, but one of the earliest and fastest post-war American sub-24-hour 100-miler. He said he walked 176,660 steps and wore out a quarter inch of his leather shoes. Smith was very proud of his walk and, like many other professional ultrarunners through time seeking fame, overstated the feat. He proclaimed that it was a world record beating a **W. F. Baker** of England who walked 100-miles in the time of 17:27:35 in 1926. (It is extremely doubtful that Smith walked strict race-walking style as Baker did and the distance was never certified.)

Smith proclaimed he was the champion distance walker in all of Oregon and was open to any challenge, at any time, for a distance of between 50 and 150 miles. In 1952 he raced **Harry Roisum (1909-1991)** from Salem to Portland and back, a distance said to be 94 miles. The heavy Labor Day holiday traffic made it a terrible experience, walking mostly on the rocky road shoulders and both quit after 80 miles in 19:08:00.

Paul Smith died in 1962 at the age of 77 of a stroke and was called "Walking Smith" in his obituary.

1952 Bath Road 100-mile Walk

100-mile walks resumed in England after World War II. On October 3, 1952, a race was conducted on the Bath Road to Chiswick, London, England called, "The Sunday Dispatch 100 Miles Open Road Walking Race." It was said to be the first point-to-point 100-mile walking race held in Great Britain. Britain's leading long-distance walkers took part, including

Olympian **George Bernard Rex Whitlock** (1910-1982) who placed fourth in the 50K walk at the 1952 Olympics in Helsinki, and won the London to Brighton Walk five times. Also in the race was 100-mile track world walking record holder, **Tom W. Richardson**, who walked 100 miles in 17:35:04 in 1936 in Bradford, England. In second place was **P. J. Reading**, with 18:18:54.

There were 52 starters who set off from Bath at 6 p.m. "Dense crowds filled the streets of Bath, and a hearty west country welcome followed the progress of the race until after midnight despite cold and fog. Very few of the competitors had dropped out at half-way."

Whitlock won in 17:44:40, missing the record by only nine minutes. 38 finished and 27 of the starters finished in less than 24 hours. With that performance, Whitlock became the 174th member of the Centurions since 1911, those who had

Rex Whitlock

walked 100-miles in less than 24 hours in a judged racewalk race.

In July 1957, the Bath to London 100-Miler was held again with 60 starters in heat and humidity. It was won by **John E. Ridley**, a 100-mile rookie in 18:12:04.

Other yearly, 100-mile walking races continued to be held. On August 7, 1953, the Road Walking Association organized a race from Birmingham to London's Wembley Stadium. It was won by **Tom Richardson** in 18:56:36.

1954 London to Brighton and Back

In 1954, the London to Brighton and Back 104-miler was held again on July 16-17. 1954. This time, it was a running race. "Mr. **Ernest Neville**, Road Runners' Club honorary secretary, is organizing the first-ever Brighton-to-London-and-Back Road Running Race. The object of the event is to set up a record time for the double course of just over 104 miles." They speculated the winner would finish in 12 to 13 hours. Nine runners started from Westminster and had to

Derek Reynolds

contend with high winds and driving rain during the night. **Derek Reynolds** (1914-1962), age 40, a clerk, a member of the Blackheath Harriers, and the English record holder for 40 and 50 miles, won in 14:54:59. **Leslie Pocock** (1926-) finished in second place with 15:22:26. Reynolds said, "Conditions were pretty tough, but I am all right. I would never contemplate running from Brighton-to-London and back again." It was the last 100-miler in his storied running career. During the past 22 years, he had never quit during a race.

March of Dimes 100-miler

In January 1955, **Dick Mitchell,** a Marine Corps recruiting sergeant in Carbondale, Illinois, went on a 100-mile hike to raise $5,000 for the March of Dimes. Mitchell, a Purple Heart veteran of the Korean War, gave himself a week to travel a highway route to 14 cities for 100 miles. "The recruiter said before his long march he was doing it to help young polio victims whose parents couldn't afford the costly treatment." He said, "I never thought this would be this big."

MARINE RESTS HIS SORE FEET

Mitchell Relaxes After His 100-Mile Walk to Help the March of Dimes

Mitchell walked in a combat uniform with a rifle slung on his shoulder. He was with donned a pair of well-broken-in GI shoes and was equipped with three pair of wool socks. He said, "I can afford a blister or two to help buy crutches for the polio kids." He returned home each night after hiking from 12 to 20 miles between cities. He went back each morning to where he had stopped the previous night.

Counting side-stops, foot races, and exhibitions, he thought he actually covered 200 miles. He reached an intersection and vowed he would not move another step until he collected $100. Mitchell's idea eventually caught on for group walks. The first March of Dimes Walkathon was held in 1958, in Tennessee.

Minnesota 100-Miler

On July 12, 1955, fifteen soldiers from Fort Carson, Colorado started a 100-mile, 60-hour hike from Brainerd, Minnesota, to the Minneapolis Aquatennial, an annual

Ft. Carson Soldiers To Stage 100-Mile Hike to Aquatennial

summer water sports festival. It included a unique way to celebrate the finish. "The troops were equipped with rifles, personal equipment and food rations, and once they reach Minneapolis, they will carry out a hit-and-run raid on a house and destroy it."

Blind Walker achieves 100 Miles

Archie Brown, a war-blinded physiotherapist from Cricklewood London, age 59, was the first known

Blind walker aspires to 100 miles in 24 hours

blind runner to achieve 100 miles in under 24 hours. He finished the 104-mile London to Brighton and Back in 1955, in 23:16:58.

Punishment 100-miler

In 1957, in Germany, eight US paratroopers became lost or went AWOL for three days while on maneuvers. To make up for the lost training and proficiency points lost to their unit, they were ordered to march 100 miles back to their barracks in Munich. Two sergeants and a chaplain marched

100-Mile Hike 'Punishment' Fine, GI's Say

with them. Six of them made it back in 46 hours with normal rest and sleep in field conditions. Only one man thought it was a rotten deal. The rest seemed to enjoy it and thought the work was justified.

100-mile Walk for Peace

In April 1958, protesters got into the 100-mile journey effort. At Philadelphia, Pennsylvania, 60 people set off on a 100-mile walk to the

United Nations headquarters in New York City to protest nuclear bomb tests that were taking place. They wanted tests to stop because of the danger of radioactive fallout. Many of the walkers brought their children along. They carried signs that read "Stop atom tests" and "Start to disarm." After the second day of 20 miles, half of them had to drop out because of jobs or schools, but 30 continued in the rain from Trenton, New Jersey. Motorists along the way were mostly encouraging and accepted pamphlets. Many with very sore feet made it and joined a group of 500 peace walkers from six states who paraded through midtown Manhattan. Four months later, the United States detonated the first nuclear weapon in outer space.

The Dutch 100-miler

1958 marked the 50th year that a 100-mile hike was held as part of a Dutch foot festival. The event was organized in 1909 with 45 hikers who made a trek around the Nijmegen countryside. For the 50th anniversary of the event, 14,000 soldiers from 12 countries and civilians made the hike under the sponsorship of the Royal Netherlands League for Physical Culture. The group hiked 25 miles for four consecutive days to reach 100 miles. Those who finished were presented with a small gilt cross.

"The network of secondary roads spreading out from Nijmegen provides a different 25-mile route for each day's march. Motorcycle squads and Dutch highway police direct the marchers, who begin and end each hike from a

central point in the heart of the city. On the final day of this year's festival, 500,000 men, women and children lined the last three miles of the route to cheer on the 12,682 bone-weary finishers."

The four-day march continues to the present and has been held for more than 100 years. In 2017, nearly 49,000 hikers participated.

100 Mile Open Road Walking Race

During the 1950s, each year a large 100-mile walking race was held in England using strict standards to qualify athletes to become Centurions. In July 1958, on one of the hottest days of the

The walker who came back
LEICESTER JOINER
WINS 100-MILER

year, a point-to-point road race was held between Leicester and Skegness, with 41 starters, put on by the walking clubs of the two cities.

Wilf Smith

The race was won by a 34-year-old joiner from Leicester, **Wilfred "Wilf" Obiss Smith** (1924-2016), who attempted the distance for the first time and finished in 18:02:37, the fifth fastest 100-mile walking time, up to that point. Two years earlier, Smith had given up walking, but was persuaded by a club committeeman to come back to the sport, train, and give the 100-miler a shot.

Smith took the lead at 30 miles and never looked back, cheered on by his wife and two of his four children. The heat took its toll on the field. "Visitors who had come into the town by coach and motorcar reported seeing athletes lying by the roadside, either resting or in a state of collapse, and others staggering dazedly, but doggedly onwards."

Thousands of spectators lined the road to the finish at the clock tower to watch the winner come in. "After passing the finishing line, Smith was surrounded by members of the St. John Ambulance Brigade, but their attentions were not necessary. A glass of milk and a kiss from his wife were sufficient to revive him before he received his trophy."

Sixty-two-year-old **William "Bill" F. Falconer** of Yorkshire met with an accident. "Just outside Boston, England, Bill was in a collision with his attendant cyclist and thrown into a bed of nettles when he injured his ankle. When he discovered that he was unable to continue, he broke down and wept. It was the first time in 37 years that he had failed to complete a 100-mile walk." Twenty-five walkers finished, with thirteen in under 24 hours, who became Centurions.

World Refugee 100

In 1959, Brian Dale, a 17-year-old grocery store assistant from Stafford, England "caught the marching bug" to walk 100 miles in 24 hours. His boss promised five pounds if he was successful, which Dale would then donate to the World Refugee Fund getting attention that year.

To train for the event, Dale went on two long walks at an average pace of seven miles an hour. For his 100-mile attempt, he set off on December 5, 1959, crewed by his cyclist friend, **Clifford Law**. "But the attempt failed ingloriously at Lichfield when he slipped on a pavement and twisted his ankle. He returned home by bus." He was still determined to try again in the future.

100-mile Love Race

In Bangor, Wales in 1960, two identical twins, **Howard Clarke** and **Vaughan Clarke**,

SHE LOVES 'EM BOTH

Twin Brothers Compete for Bride Prize in 100-Mile Walking Match

age 19, staged a 100-mile walking race for the hand of a 19-year-old college student they both loved. **Jean Gowan** just could not decide which one to marry. Jean finally decided the two electronics engineering students should hold a gentlemanly contest to settle her indecision once and for all.

She met the two at a university dance. "From then on, she'd date first one and then the other and sometimes couldn't be sure which one had showed up to take her out. When the dating blossomed into love, well, things got more confusing by the moment."

Jean said, "I love them both. We have thought carefully about who my future husband might be, but we think this is the best way. The winner can take me to the school ball on Saturday, then we'll get the engagement ring."

All three insisted the contest was not a publicity stunt, and that they were doing it for love, not money. They said if they ended up in a tie, that they would try something else, perhaps a boxing match. The course was from Bangor to Flint and back.

She met the two at a university dance. "From then on, she'd date first one and then the other and sometimes couldn't be sure which one had showed up to take her out. When the dating blossomed into love, well, things got more confusing by the moment."

The race began on February 19, 1960. After waving a scarf at the town clock and murmuring, "May the best man win", Jean jumped into an automobile and followed for a short distance. But she returned to Bangor,

expecting to greet the winner when they returned sometime the next day.

True Love Foiled!

Coeds Kidnap Twin Racing Brother for Girl's Hand

The twins were allowed to walk or run. After they reached Colwyn Bay, at about the 20-mile mark, **Vaughan Clarke** was grabbed by students packed into a waiting car who kidnapped him. Howard then quit the race and said, "This has wrecked all our plans." It was believed that Vaughan was taken to the Liverpool Campus by students who were opposed to the gamble for the lady. Jean was in a quandary and said, "All this does is increase the suspense and frustrate us all. I do hope Vaughan will be returned so he can continue the race. I do hope Vaughan is safe. I love them both."

It was reported that the whole thing might have been a hoax and connected to "Rag Week" when students perform stunts to raise money for charity. Vaughn was released, and an abbreviated version of the race was then scheduled but stopped when parents of the three stepped in. They said no engagement would take place. The three soon admitted that the "love race" was a hoax, and that they did it as a publicity stunt to put Bangor on the map.

100 miles on a Bet

In September 1960, **Bartholomew "Bart" Barror** (1932-1993), age 28, of Assumption, Illinois, a former high school football hero, and Korea War veteran, boasted to friends that it would be easy to walk 100 miles in 40 hours. His friends were sure he couldn't and put up $250 against his success. Barror measured out a two-mile course and started at 6 a.m. one morning.

After eleven and a half hours, he had covered 36 miles and was still on schedule. His wife wanted him to stop and said, "He's getting awfully tired. I didn't want him to take the bet, but I thought he could do it. He doesn't care too much about the money, he just wanted show his friends that he could win." Barror quit just a half hour later at 12 hours. He said, "The first twenty miles were a breeze, but after that, the going was rough." He thought a younger man could do it.

CHAPTER THIRTEEN

Padre Island 110-Miler

What was the first American ultradistance race in the modern post-war era? Perhaps the answer is the "Padre Island Walkathon" 110-miler, a three-day stage race that was started in 1953. While it wasn't a pure 100-mile race because participants stopped each night, it was very forward-thinking and incorporated many of the practices later used in 100-mile races such as runner tracking, real-time reporting, and aid stations.

This unusual race was a point-to-point race that ran along the sandy beaches of the Gulf of Mexico in Texas. Previously long endurance races were mostly limited to professionals. This race was for everyone, the old, the young teenagers, and even women during an era when female participation in endurance events was viewed as inappropriate.

About Padre Island

Padre Island, about 113 miles long, is the longest barrier island in the world. This long, skinny, sandy island is the second largest island by area in the lower-48 states. Only Long Island in New York tops it. In 1908, the first development was established on the island, the Gulf-Side Casino Hotel, near the southern tip of the island. But the hotel received serious damage from storms and hurricanes over the years. For many years, it was closed to make repairs. A storm took the top story of the hotel off in 1945, and they demolished the entire structure in the early 1950s.

The Padre Island Causeway

Around 1930, they built a causeway to connect Corpus Christi to the northern end of the island, allowing access to the Gulf's beaches. During World War II, they used the northern section of the island as a bombing range. By 1953, the island was again undeveloped and used almost exclusively by ranchers. It wasn't until 1970 that development started again.

Founding the Race

In 1951, **Cash Ervin Asher** (1891-1984), a journalist and author, was the publicity man for the Padre Island Park Board and the causeway. He likely came up with the idea to hold the race and became the race director. The aim was to walk the length of the island end-to-end. This would be a way to get more publicity for the island and thus attract tourists.

CASH ASHER.

Asher named the race "Padre Island Walkathon." The term ultramarathon would not be used until 1964. The term "walkathon" was being used for any long walking event. Why walk and not run? In the 1950s in America, people considered running ultra distances to be inconceivable. They advertised the race and opened registration in early 1953.

Race Format

The format for the event was a three-day staged race from the south tip of the island to the northern end, a distance of about 110 miles. The contestants would walk on no roads, just beaches and sandy tracks pounded down by vehicles. This certainly was a *trail* ultramarathon.

For the first year, the walkers would cover 25 miles the first day, 42 miles the second day, and 43 miles on the last day. They would all camp at the start and also for each night after days one and two. A large support caravan of vehicles would go along with the walkers, providing food, medical treatment, news coverage, and transportation for those who could not continue. If a walker dropped out, they were expected to continue with the caravan to the finish. Entrants would be provided tents.

The rules were pretty simple. Running was prohibited. The published rules stated, "anyone caught running will be thrown out of the race." Beer or hard liquor were also prohibited during the race. Anyone who partook would be disqualified automatically.

The event was scheduled to start on Friday, March 27, 1953, and would end on Sunday evening. The race filled up with 70 daring starters. None of them had any genuine experience with this kind of event. They would learn "on the job." The start location was at the southern tip of the island, near Port Isabel. The finish line was 110 miles to the north at Bob Hall Fishing Pier in Gulf Park, across from Corpus Christi, Texas.

The 1953 Contestants

Reverend J. D. Holland

Tiny Thompson

The oldest walker was 67 years old, and the youngest starter was fifteen. **Reverend J. D. Holland** was a 67-year-old minister of Christ Church in Port Isabel, a small community across the water from the start. He was an experienced walker and tried to train for the event. About a week before the race, he walked from Port Isabel to Brownsville, a distance of 30 miles, and reported that he "wasn't a bit tired" when he finished. Reverend Holland said he entered the contest "because at one time, when his health was broken, and he recovered by walking." He said, "I want to convince my grandchildren that they can come back after being very ill if they have the will do so."

Another unusual contestant was **Tiny Thompson**, a 417-pound taxicab driver from Brownsville, Texas. He was confident and said, "If my 'dogs' hold out, I'll finish right up front."

A boy scout patrol from Edinburg, Texas was entered. Several young scouts with their leader took up the challenge. There was no discrimination against women, at least eleven were in the field and an award of $100 was put up by a local business for the first woman finisher.

1953 Race Preparation

All contestants were asked to camp out the night before at the start. Those coming from the north, near Corpus Christi, were provided transportation to the start. They met at 1 p.m. on Thursday, at the Padre Island Causeway near Corpus Christi. They were given rides across the causeway and were driven down the beach, 110 miles, to the starting place on the southern tip of the island. Vehicles used were cars, jeeps, pickups and converted Army ambulances. Those coming from the south, near Brownsville,

Chow Wagon

took a ferry across the water to the start camp (There was no causeway there yet). That night at camp, a doctor checked out all the contestants. A member of the Red Cross would watch their health and pull them out of the race if needed.

Small airplanes were used to fly news copy, photos, and radio recordings to Corpus Christi, and bring back supplies. A Ham radio operator traveled with the walkers and stayed in contact with the mainland. He was a member of the Corpus Christi Radio Club. The radio team on the mainland could relay real-time news to the public and families.

Day One - 1953

The race started at 8:30 a.m. with 70 starters beginning their 25-mile day-one quest. The ocean views were incredible, but the contestants quickly learned how tiring it was to walk in the sand. To make matters worse, the constant wind blew the sand everywhere. Sunburn was avoided by most of the walkers who wore long sleeves, long pants, sun "helmets" or caps, "and smeared protective oils on their hands and faces." The ham radio guy reported that about 20 out of the field of 70 did little walking and soon quit. The support vehicles had challenges with continual mechanical troubles.

The destination for the day-one camp was on the beach near the wreck of the *SS Nicaragua*. In 1912, the *SS Nicaragua*, a cargo ship, left Tampico, Mexico, with a cargo of cotton and other items. It was bound for Port Arthur, Texas. Five days later a terrible storm sank vessels all over the Gulf of Mexico and the *Nicaragua* ran aground at Devil's Elbow, a site where many shipwrecks occurred over the years. The wreck could be seen at low tide.

SS Nicaragua run aground on Padre Island
Photo taken 1913

Photo taken in early 1930's

Photo taken in 2012

Day 1 women leaders, Winnie Beth Brillhard, and Bonnie White. with Roger Oswalt, high school student

Jesse Gaylor Shamblin (1911-1978) a 42-year-old plant worker from McAllen, Texas, finished day one in first place with 5:32 for the 25-mile segment. **Bonnie White**, an employee at the Naval Air Station and **Winnie Beth Brillhart** (1912-1996), 41-year-old mother of four adult children, tied with 6:40.

More than half the field, 40 of 70, didn't make it to the day-one camp and were given rides to the wreck site. All the walkers were supposed to stay and ride with the company, but one runner dropping out (DNF) insisted on being given a ride off the island and left early. All others stayed to cheer on the remaining walkers. Most of them established a close

Four scouts finished Day 1 and waited for their leader to finish

friendship as they traveled and camped each night. It was uncomfortably cold during the night.

Day Two - 1953

Twenty-nine contestants showed up for the day two start at 6:45 a.m. **Alice Chappell** didn't start because of a severe blister. Many courageous walkers who started the day two stage of 42 miles admitted they doubted they would make it to the next camp near Yarborough Pass. As they were walking along that day, **Frank Jurecko** (1920-1974) found a message in a bottle that had washed ashore on the sands and considered that a "good omen." **Ricky Lutz**

Robbie Pope on right getting some feet treatment by the Red Cross volunteer

used a walking stick and was nicknamed by his fellow-walkers, "The sheepherder."

Day two took a heavy toll as 20 walkers didn't make it all the way to camp and dropped out. Nine finished day two, including two women who called it quits at that point, mile 67. Both were tied in time, the last two women in the competition, so they split the $100 award. They were **Robbie**

Pope (1934-2011), (18) of Port Isabel, Texas, and **Winnie Beth Brillhart** (41) of Corpus Christi, Texas. Pope said, "Next year we'll know what we're up against on this sand. Next year I'll finish the walk."

Day Three Finish - 1953

Six contestants started day three and walked up and over Yarborough Pass. **Clifford Templemand** (1933-1957), a college student, gave up after six miles. Two others soon also dropped out during the grueling 43-mile final segment. Three remained and continued to the 110-mile finish at Bob Hall Fishing Pier in Gulf Park.

In first place was **Jesse Shamblin**, age 42, of McAllen, Texas, with a total walking time of 28:48. He won $250. In second place was **Frank Jurecko**, age 32, of Corpus Christi, Texas, with a total walking time of 31:14. He won $50. Amazingly, in third place was fifteen-year-old boy scout, **Charles Bolton** (1933-1983) of Corpus Christi. He won $40. Those that didn't finish day two and three mostly had blister problems. They learned that the type of shoe worn was very important. The three finishers wore leather, solid shoes. Frank and Jesse wore high-top leather shoes.

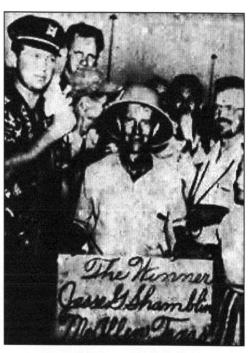

The winner, Jesse Shamblin

Jurecko took a day off work but returned two days after finishing. He said he was "pretty stiff and sore" with a swollen ankle, and some blisters. His wife said, "The boys at the plant told him to come on and they would carry him around so he wouldn't have to miss work."

Race Director, **Cash Asher**, thought the event was a great success. Talking about the race volunteers and walkers who didn't finish: "And I tell you that is the best bunch of people I've ever met in my life. Everybody pitched in and helped where they were needed." A reunion was planned for two months later on the island at Gulf Park. The 1953 Padre Island Walkathon created quite a stir in Texas, opening minds to what truly was possible. Covering ultra distances could be accomplished by non-professionals.

The 1954 Race

For the 1954 Padre Island Walkathon, the segments for each day were adjusted to 40, 40, and 30 miles. The starters more than doubled to 148 contestants. The race got a lot of attention. Sponsors came forward. 7-Up Bottling Company furnished a truck to serve soft drinks along the way. A trucking company provided a wrecker to tow out any vehicles stuck in the sand. A local hotel provided all the meals for the contestants and staff from a mobile kitchen that was moved from camp to camp. The support crew that year included about 50 vehicles with medics, cooks, and record keepers.

The entry fee was $10. Each contestant needed to bring their own bedding, cot, and tent. The Race Director emphasized the race was hard and predicted that only about 13 of the 148 would finish. "It's a long walk and only those who have trained for the event will have a chance of reaching the finish lines."

1954 Contestants

Defending champion **Jess Shamblin** returned along with eight other race veterans, including 16-year-old boy scout, **Charles Bolton**, and 68-year-old **Reverend Holland**. That year, the contestants took training much more seriously and regularly trained walking on the island to get used to the sand.

Sergeant Rand Tellez, of the State Guard Reserve Corps, registered with a month to go. He immediately stopped smoking and started to walk 12 miles round trip each day to work.

Brothers R.C. and Floyd Aexander train on the Padre Island Beach.

With a week to go, he did a 45-mile walk without food or water to make sure he could at least handle the first day of the race. Tellez was a 29-year-old father of seven children and served in World War II on an aircraft carrier. He admitted he didn't walk much on the ship.

The Course Was the Story That Year

By doubling the field in 1954, race director **Cash Asher** more than doubled the risk by growing the field too fast. Yes, he did bring in much more help, but the race that year turned into a race director's nightmare.

More news coverage came out that year. A local TV station covered the start. Two

Ham radio operators check out their equipment

radio stations would tape segments for their broadcasts. Life magazine sent out a photographer to cover the race for their new sports magazine.

Soon after the start, terrible thunderstorms rolled in with hail and high winds. Sand pounded both walkers and cars. The walkers were miserable, and they missed lunch when the lunch jeep didn't arrive because of the poor conditions. To make matters worse, the supply vehicle got stuck in the sand and the contestants who made it to the day-one finish had to wait until 9 p.m. for dinner. Only 77 out of 148 arrived in time.

On day-two, the course was the story. The beach was in the worst condition that locals had ever seen. **Cash Asher** claimed that the Padre Island Walkathon "is the toughest, roughest athletic contest in the world." That day it probably was. The beach was soft and covered with seaweed in most

Big Shell

places. The "Big Shell" section was covered with shells, making it the roughest section. In that segment, many of the supply vehicles containing tents, cots, bedrolls and 500 gallons of water bogged down and got stuck. The tow truck consumed so much gas trying to free vehicles that there wasn't enough gas for the tow truck, leaving other vehicles stranded.

Despite the challenging conditions, **James B. "J.B." Outlaw** (1918-2004) a high school track coach, age 35, was able to set a blistering pace on day one and continued it on day two, averaging better than 4.5 miles per hour. His total time for 80 miles was 17:23. He and the walker in second place arrived at the day-two camp ahead of the support vehicles in the terrible conditions. Both claimed they had no blisters and no sore muscles.

Only 29 of the 148 starters reached camp on day two by 8 p.m., which was the cutoff. The defending champions, **Jesse Shamblin** and **Beth Brillhart,** were among the DNF casualties. Alarmingly, the equipment truck, with tents and food, was nowhere in sight. Without tents, the contestants huddled around small fires and wrapped themselves in blankets. Spectators who had extra picnic food supplied emergency food. The 7-Up truck saved the day by picking up a huge amount of cooked meat, sandwiches and eggs when it went into Corpus Christi to get a new supply of soft drinks. It arrived into the camp at 9 p.m. The equipment truck with the tents finally arrived at 11 p.m. Morale was boosted that year by using a generator for light. The previous year, they only had bonfires and flashlights.

Only nineteen contestants started day three. Outlaw went on to win the event with a sub-24 time of 23:45. But it was very close. Second place was just 8 minutes behind. The women's winner was **Erna Lietzenburg**, an employee at the local Naval Air Station. She won a clothes dryer. Sixteen-year-old **Charles Bolton** finished in 29:40. **Sergeant Tellez** finished in 32:31. He walked half the course barefoot after saltwater drenched his shoes. **Floyd Alexander**, one of the brother's team, finished in 28:16. Of the 148 starters, fifteen men and one woman finished all three days.

The champion, Outlaw, said of his race experience, "it was as much a mental and emotional strain as a physical one." Decades later, he was still proud of this accomplishment, calling it his most prized victory of his lifetime, as he looked upon more than 100 trophies he won for running victories over the years.

Lietzenburg, the woman's winner, mentioned how lonely it was at times, not seeing another walker in either direction. Another walker said, "and when it rained Friday and the thunder was crashing and lightning was flashing all around and you couldn't see any distance ahead, you began to wonder if you would come out alive."

The disasters weren't over. More than 2,000 cars made the trip over the causeway on Sunday to witness the finish and watch a beauty pageant. That caused a massive traffic jam getting to and from the island.

The 1955 Race

Jack Sanders took over as the race director. Only 68 contestants started as interest was waning. The event was being billed as "the toughest 100-mile walking contest in the world." Reporters from 20 magazines and newspapers were on hand that year to cover the race. Support vehicles included six four-wheel vehicles, and four mule-drawn wagons that were

used to pick up the walkers that dropped out. Boy scouts rode in the wagons to provide first aid. To make things much easier, they put ten 50-gallon water kegs at various places along the course, so they didn't have to haul them for the entire 110 miles. 60 members of the local Ham radio club took part. Twenty planes flew cover for the event, transporting newspaper and radio releases and were ready for emergencies.

A stuck mule wagon being pulled out of the sand by a truck

Joyce Wickham

Day one was very hot, causing many contestants to drop out. Walkers were motivated seeing a 7-up soft drink truck in the distance that supplied cold drinks and salt tablets. Yes, even in 1955, they understood the importance of salt. After day one, **Charlie Riley**, a 27-year-old insurance salesman and high school track coach had the lead. He had prepared by walking hundreds of miles. The day-three start format was changed that year. The leader, Charlie, started at 7:00 a.m., but the other walkers' start time was determined by how far they were behind Charlie. He finished in first with a new course record, a very impressive 20:59. Twelve finished. Charlie won $500 and a used car.

Joyce Wickham, age 23, a draftsman for an oil company, set the women's course record 27:50 and was sixth overall. She won $250 and an automatic washing machine. About 15,000 spectators lined the beach at the finish. Instead of a belt buckle, all the finishers were awarded a cigarette lighter with "Padre Island Walkathon" and their finish place engraved on it.

The 1956 Race

The 4th annual edition of the Padre Island Walkathon had 61 starters with 7 women. The overall winners of the previous years were all in the event, **Jesse Shamblin, J.B. Outlaw**, and **Charlie Riley**. It was announced that **Sammy Baugh** (1914-2008) a famous quarterback for the Washington Redskins from 1937 to 1952, was the referee for the event. His plane ended up being delayed, and he didn't fire the starting gun. Riley held the lead each day and bested his own 1955 110-mile course record by 56 minutes with 20:03. He averaged nearly 6 mph for his last 30 miles. He said, "I lost seven toenails. It's the pressure from walking, the blood builds up under the nails, then you have to put a hole in them to relieve the pressure. They fall off later." 1953 champion, Shamblin came in third. **Dale Cole** walked the entire course barefoot.

Changed to a One-day 40-Miler

The race wasn't held in 1957 because it lacked a title sponsor. The Port Mansfield channel was dug without a bridge cutting the island in half, so the 1958 event was trimmed to a one-day 40-mile event, an out-and back from Bob Hall Pier to Caldwell Pier at Port Arkansas and back, which greatly simplified the support that was needed. The difficult Big Shell section was no longer a part of the race, making it easier. Newspapers started calling the event, "the wackiest walking event."

Charlie Riley again entered. He trained hard. He said, "I figure I'll have done 800 miles or more in training before the day of the race. And when I'm not training, I usually run a mile and a half every morning." The reason he was so fast was that he developed his own style and thought he could walk a 6:30 mile at full speed. Riley explained his strategy for the 40-miler. "It depends on the compaction. I'd like to set a steady pace, but I'm not going to let anybody get far ahead of me. If someone wants to set a fast pace in the first 20 miles, I'm going to keep up with him." Riley wore soft leather shoes with "crepe soles," shorts, a T-shirt, and a billed cap. Riley again won the event.

Charlie Riley

They established the first modern aid stations in ultramarathon history instead of using so many support vehicles following along. The stations were provided at 2.5-mile intervals. Food provided that year included sandwiches, chocolate, orange slices and salt tablets.

1959-1969 events

In 1959, the event had lost a lot of steam. Only about 20 walkers signed up and the distance was still 40 miles. But it still was a huge spectator event, mostly because The Miss Padre Island Pageant was part of the festivities. It was getting most of the attention in the press. Because of the small walker field, spectators were permitted to drive along the beach with the walkers but feeding them was strictly forbidden. During the 1960 race, someone went out and stole three of the water station cans. Emergency arrangements were made to get drinking water for the participants. In 1961, only about 15 walkers entered. The 1964 event was the 10th edition of the race. The Corpus Christi Junior Chamber of Congress was in charge, and they organized a beach party stretching the length of the course. A 100-mile boat race event was added, going up and down the coast. Three thousand treasure cans were dumped in the ocean to be claimed by spectators when they washed up on the island. All the events totally overshadowed the walkathon. They held a massive hot dog roast in the evening.

In 1965, only 15 walkers entered. The winner of the very first Padre Island Walkathon in 1953, **Jesse Shambin**, won for the third year in a row. He trained to tolerate dehydration and did not waste time stopping for water until mile 20. He also walked the entire 40 miles without eating at the aid stations. Over the years, he had perfected his walking form. He said, "It's second nature." He held the 40-mile course record with 7:08, set in 1959. One year a dog took away his win. "A dog running loose on the beach took a chunk out of my leg. It kind of slowed me down." He mentioned what he

Jesse Shamblin

wore, "I wear shorts, a sports shirt, light leather shoes and anchor supports for my socks, so they won't slip down around my heels and start raising blisters."

1969 was the last year that the Padre Island Walkathon was held. It appears that none of the elite walkers became ultrarunners and that the race probably didn't really influence future ultras, but it was fascinating to see how a supported trail ultra race developed over the years with aid stations. It also demonstrated to the public and participants that you didn't have to be a professional athlete to achieve results that are amazing.

CHAPTER FOURTEEN

1957 Utah Man vs. Horse 157-Miler

For more than two centuries, people have debated if humans on foot could beat horses. Those on the side of humans argued that over a long enough distance, such as 100 miles, human beings could outrun horses. "It has been contended that humans are capable of covering vast distances after the horse becomes winded and unable to continue."

To prove this point, ultradistance races billed as "Man vs. Horse" were competed as early as 1879. But it was a long-forgotten 157-mile "man vs. horse" race held in Utah, in 1957-58, that captured the attention of America and beyond. During the late 1950s, it brought the spotlight on the difficulty of running 100 miles.

19th Century

In 1879, two of the greatest pedestrians in history, **Edward Payson Weston** (1839–1929) and **Daniel O'Leary** (1841-1933) speculated how a man would do against a horse in a 6-day event. They disagreed on this subject. O'Leary believed horses would win. Weston was on the side of humans. To settle the debate, a race was held in San Francisco, California, beginning on October 15, 1879, with seven men against eleven horses on a track at Mechanics' Pavilion. A horse named *Pinafore* won with 557 miles, but there were no truly elite runners/walkers in the event.

Weston was still unconvinced, so O'Leary put on a 6.5-day event in Chicago starting on September 5, 1880. There was a crowd of four thousand spectators on hand for the first day. Five days in, **Michael J. Byrne** (1851-1927), and Irish-American from Buffalo, New York, took the lead. The leading horse was a black mare named *Betsy Baker*. On that day, she "failed to respond to the whip" and went in for two hours before she could come out again. She had finally responded to a "dose of champagne." But after that, she could do only a slow walk. Byrne won, covering 578 miles in 6.5 days. *Betsy Baker* finished in second with 563 miles.

Utah's 1957 Man vs. Horse 157-mile race

In 1957 the country turned its attention to rural Utah "to pit endurance against speed," men against horses. The 1957 contest was between two men and two horses from downtown Salt Lake City to the rural ranching/oil town of Roosevelt, in eastern Utah, a distance of about 157 miles. The course went south, up Provo Canyon to Heber City and then on Highway 40 to Roosevelt. It started at 4,300 feet and reached as high as 8,000 feet at Daniels Pass.

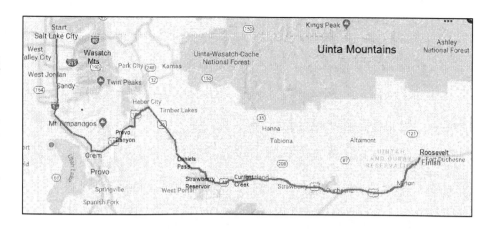

The runners chosen for this race were elite college distance runners on the Brigham Young University (BYU) track team. They were **Albert Ray** (age 24) of St. Albans, Queens, New York, and **Terry Jensen** (age 18) of Idaho Falls, Idaho. Ray was confident. "I think we'll beat them. The asphalt will be murder on the horses' feet."

BYU track coach, **Clarence Robison** (1923-2006), who ran BYU track in 1948 and went to the London Olympics that year, predicted that his runners would win in 30-36 hours on the all-pavement course. He said that if the course was instead less than 75 miles, the horse probably could win, but beyond that the advantage leans toward humans who have greater recuperative powers. He also pointed out that the runners could eat and drink on the run.

The riders were **Roy Hatch** (age 71) (1881-1959), a rancher, and **Ray Hall** (age 18) (1939-1988), an oil worker, both of Roosevelt. Hatch rode a 6-year-old thoroughbred-quarter horse. Hall rode a small 11-year-old wild Mustang that he had caught two years earlier and trained for the race.

The race was sponsored by the Roosevelt Bullberry Boys Booster Club and part of a "Days of 1906" celebration marking the opening of the nearby Ute-Ouray Indian reservation and the settling of Roosevelt, Utah. The club was led

Ray Hall

211

by **Lynn Odean Whitlock** (1901-1962) who contacted many television and radio networks about the event, putting the little town of Roosevelt on the nation's map. Stories were published as far away as Venezuela and Panama.

Sheriff fires starting gun in Salt Lake City for the 1957 "Man vs Horse" race

The race started on South Temple Street in downtown Salt Lake City near the Brigham Young monument on November 15, 1957. The contestants first paraded through downtown for five blocks where a ribbon was cut by the city mayor, and the sheriff fired a gun officially to start the race. Jeeps pulling trailers were provided as crew vehicles. Light snow fell, and the forecast was for snowy weather during the race. The track men donned blue sweat suits and covered their heads with woolen khaki, exposing only their eyes and noses to protect them from the cold.

Betting was part of the event. With one dollar, a person could put in a winning time prediction with the hope of winning a $500 US Savings bond. Profits went to a new rodeo arena for Roosevelt.

After about two hours, they reached nearby Sandy. The runners were about 1.5 miles ahead of the horses. BYU track coach Robison drove along with the runners crewing them. A BYU professor in the Health Education Department had tests performed on the runners during the race, including electrocardiograms, blood tests, and urinalyses. He said, "it isn't very often that we have an opportunity to study body functions of a man who has run 100 miles."

That night, runner Jensen dropped out about the 55-mile mark along the Deer Creek reservoir up Provo Canyon because of a tight leg tendon. The other runner, Ray, slept for about 2.5 hours during the early morning at about the 70-mile mark in Heber City and was in excellent condition. The horses had the lead and were re-shoed. As for the human shoes, Ray tried various shoes to help his feet. One pair were shoes used by marathoners had thin soles with "rippled rubber" lugs added. This type of shoe was developed for paratroopers "to lessen the shock of hitting the ground."

Ray reached the 100-mile mark in about 35 hours. Coach Robison ran along, pacing him at times during the second night. At about mile 110, with about 48 miles to go, Ray rested for 90 minutes at Current Creek, but shortly thereafter gave up the race because he was hobbling on swollen ankles. He was clearly under-trained for ultradistances. He said, "I caught up with the horses at Current Creek and felt fine except for my feet and ankles. I was forced to quit because the doctors were afraid that blood poisoning was starting to develop in the legs." Ray was later taken to the hospital in Roosevelt, and then transferred to the BYU health

Albert Ray with wrapped swollen ankles recovering in the BYU Health Center

center and treated for his swollen ankles. Ray said, "I'll be back again."

The two horses ridden by Hatch and Hall went on together. They eventually trotted down main street in Roosevelt, and broke a ribbon that stretched across an intersection to the cheers of more than 6,000 people. They finished in a very slow time of 57:15. Their actual riding time was 32:15. At times, the horses were so exhausted that they refused to eat. Hatch said, "I never had such a thrill as when someone from Salt Lake City called me Roy Rogers. The only thing is, I don't think Trigger could have made the run."

The winner of the $500 Savings bond was a man from Orem, Utah, who guessed the finishing time within about 11 minutes.

A few months later, in 1958, a Utah editorial was critical of the race and plans for a second race that year. "The man vs. horse race is a nice publicity stunt. However, over the Salt Lake to Roosevelt course, it proves little—except that both horse and man get lame pounding the paved roads."

1958 Race

The 1958 event was planned for July 22, 1958. Thirty-five runners applied to take part. They selected three runners, all professionals, **Paul "Hardrock" Simpson** (1904-1978), age 53, a mailman from Burlington, North Carolina. Simpson was a 1929 Bunion Derby (trans-USA) finisher who also raced against a horse in 1927. Also running was **Edo Romagnoli** (1921-2021), age 37, a

New York City policeman who had won multiple marathons. The final runner in the threesome was the famous one-armed runner, **Roy McMurtry** (1895-1961), age 62, of Tucson, Arizona, who had also walked the Padre Island Walkathon in Texas. In 1922, he rode a bicycle from Indianapolis to Los Angeles in 20 days.

The horsemen were **Willis Little Jacobsen** (1897-1990), age 61, of West Jordan, Utah on an Arabian stallion, **Keith Bastian** (1936-2019), age 21, who substituted for his father, of Neola, Utah on a thoroughbred quarter horse, and University of Utah student, **Joseph Stewart "Stew" Paulick** (1934-) age 24, of Tooele, Utah, riding on a thoroughbred, *Dodger*.

Jeeps pulling trailers were again provided for each participant to carry food and medical supplies and to provide a resting place for runners and riders.

PARADE – Salt Lake City – starting at 9 a.m. near the Brigham Young Monument, and ending at Fifth South and Main Street.

—1—

Race Course will follow Highway 91 to Orem, then to Heber City where it will proceed to Roosevelt via Highway 40.

—1—

HARDROCK SIMPSON
Burlington, N. C.
Mail carrier—walks 12 miles daily. He is world's champion runner, great track coach, and North Carolina's top home-grown athlete. In 1927 he outran a horse 25 miles over 140-mile course.

Race will be patrolled by Salt Lake County and Duchesne County Sheriff Departments from Salt Lake City to Roosevelt.

ROY MCMURTRY
Tucson, Arizona
Roy was 1928 Indiana Marathon Champion. In 1922 rode bicycle from Indianapolis to Los Angeles in 20 days. Finished among top 10 in world's Walkathon at Padre Island, Texas.

Can Man Conquer Horse This Year? What's your guess in this race?

Secure Guessing Tickets from all Utah American Legion Posts or members; the Roosevelt Chamber of Commerce; or from Bullberry Boys.

—1—

● GRAND PRIZE ●
$500.00 U. S. SAVINGS BOND
For Person Making Best Guess !

—1—

— For information on —
$10,000 TRAILRIDE
September 2, 1958 — Write:
BULLBERRY BOYS BOOSTER
CLUB - ROOSEVELT, UTAH

EDO ROMAGNOLI
New York City, N. Y.
Is a patrolman on New York City Police Force. Ranked among top distance runners. Edo has won many medals and set many records. He finished high in Boston Marathon on April 8, 1958.

A masked "mystery" rider known as "The Bat," who wasn't entered in the race, showed up at the start. He was clothed in a black flowing robe and helmet. "The Bat" rode up on a "skittish" cow pony painted with white circles. He was an unwelcome participant and organizer **Lynn Whitlock** said, "When he gets to Roosevelt, we'll rip that mask right off." The "Bat" didn't say a word at the start. "The rimless spectacles perched outside the mask glinting over its eye holes."

Before the actual start, the participants paraded five blocks in downtown Salt Lake City led by native Americans from the Ute and Ouray reservation, performing tribal dances at the middle of each block and at each intersection.

A teenager, **Val Sharp**, on a long-distance bike, also joined the procession just south of Salt Lake

"The Bat" on his painted horse. Evidently, he changed to white on the very hot day

City and tagged along for another 50 miles before tiring out at Heber. "The tourists piled up behind the riders and runners as they headed east from

Orem, abandoning four-lane for two-lane pavement. For all of it, they were patient, if somewhat bewildered. Hardly a horn honked and sheriff's deputies shepherding the caravan waved them by at every wide spot of the road."

Romagnoli led the race for the first few hours, but then "The Bat" overtook him. McMurtry made it to about mile 25, dropping out three miles north of Lehi. He said, "I had cramps in my leg, and they seemed to get worse all the time. This'll be my last run. At 62, I think I'm just a bit too old."

In Orem, Hardrock Simpson's escort Jeep missed the turn toward Provo Canyon and led him four miles out of his way into Provo. When the mistake was discovered, the Jeep driver tried to convince Simpson to take a ride back to the missed turn, but Simpson refused to take a ride and ran back to the mistake point, running eight "bonus miles."

It was 90 degrees as they made their way up Provo Canyon, scattered across ten miles. At the junction in Heber to turn onto Highway 40, there were about 3,000 spectators cheering the racers.

That evening, Romagnoli took a two-hour rest stop in Heber. He vowed, "I'll go on 'till I fall on my face.'" He was treated like a hero "through towns along the race route and drew cheers and applause. Patrons of a café in Heber City, where he stopped for two glasses of water Tuesday night, rose and applauded as he entered."

"The Bat" dropped out about mile 85 at Strawberry Reservoir. His horse was exhausted, and it refused to go further. (Later, they identified "The Bat" as **Kenneth Higley** (1925-2006), of Salt Lake City. He was a World War II veteran pilot and was age 32 at the time with a wife and several children).

Kenneth "The Bat" Higley in later years

Paulick took over the lead as his horse, *Dodger,* had renewed strength. Paulick explained, "He started running like he usually does, and that's when we made our time." When Romagnoli reached the high point of the course, Daniels Summit, near Strawberry Reservoir, there were no hot drinks there as he had expected, and he was chilled for the rest of the night. He said, "Even though it was all downhill, my legs were chilled and aching and I couldn't run."

Romagnoli, far ahead of the other runners, made it down from Strawberry Reservoir and hit the 100-mile mark at 21:22, which that year was the fastest known time for 100 miles in the modern (post-war) American ultrarunning era. He continued and at about 6 a.m., he was given a hot bath at Currant Creek. They drew a small cup of blood from blood blisters beneath two toenails. (He later lost six toenails.) The bath seemed to hurt more than help because it drained his remaining strength. He said, "I could feel it coming and knew after two miles I didn't have any bounce and wouldn't be able to finish." He dropped out at about mile 118 because of severe cramping and at the recommendation of a doctor. At the time, he was only about two miles behind the leading horse (Paulick on *Dodger*) and well ahead of the other remaining horses and runner in the race.

For the last 20 miles of the race, driving rain pounded the leader, Paulick on *Dodger.* It was the first rain in that area in 2 ½ months.

Paulick entered the little town of Roosevelt, cheered by about 2,000 people jamming Main Street, and finished on *Dodger* in 29:33:40, beating the remaining runner, Simpson, by 57 miles. During his ride, Paulick made six rest stops, totaling about three and a half hours. He reported that he had stiff legs and was eager to get into dry clothes. Paulick said that *Dodger* trotted about 90 percent of the time. *Dodger* was ready to drop at the finish but was quickly led off for feed, water, and a rubdown. (The vets would declare the next day that he was in sound condition. In 2023, **Joseph Stewart "Stew" Paulick** was 89 years old and still living in Tooele, Utah).

Race organizer, Whitlock proclaimed, "Horses have proven, for the second time in less than a year, that man is no match in a long race." Romagnoli, who at the finish line, agreed that "man will invariably come in second in an endurance race. Everyone knows a horse can run faster than a man, but the theory was that the horse would wear out over a prolonged route, but they don't." Romagnoli also said, "I don't think anyone ever ran 100 miles like that before. You could go all over the world and not find a course as rough as that. I made a good race while I was in it."

Whitlock announced that this race was the last "Man vs Horse" race to be put on by his group. "After a race using amateur runners and one using professional runners, we feel it has been decided definitely that a horse can outrun a man over a 157-mile course."

After Paulick finished, Simpson, at mile 100, was told the race was over and that he needed to stop. Simpson vowed he wouldn't quit until he reached Roosevelt. Officials ordered the removal of his escort jeep and formally declared the race was finished. But Simpson continued to run, with his wife driving along in a station wagon. A few hours later, as evening arrived, Simpson decided to quit after reaching 118 miles, stopping at the same point that Romagnoli had reached. Rider, **Willis Jacobsen,** also continued. He managed to finish at Roosevelt during the night about ten hours after Paulick, in about 39 hours.

A few weeks later, **Edo Romagnoli** was on the TV program, "To Tell the Truth," to pick the right person who ran against the horses. In 2021, Romagnoli died at 99 years old in Florida.

In October 1959, **Alva Leroy Hatch**, a horseman finisher of the 1957 race, went missing on a scheduled bus trip from Long Beach, California, to Durango, Colorado. His body was found four months later near Farmington, New Mexico. Family members said that 73-year-old Hatch liked to "roam around and prospect." They believed that he experienced a heart attack. Foul play was ruled out.

CHAPTER FIFTEEN

Ron Hopcroft and Jackie Mekler

Ronald Frederick Hopcroft (1918-2016) was born in Cheswick, England and was active in many sports as a schoolboy. He competed in cross-country and track races before being called into the service during World War II. After returning, he started running long-distance on roads in 1949 at the age of 31. In the early 1950s he started running in ultra-distance races in England, including London to Brighton, where he won in 1956 in 5:36:25.

100 Mile World Record

Hopcroft, like the ultrarunners before him, wanted to go after the world record 100-mile time on Bath Road from Box to London. He knew that Wally Hayward set the record in 1953 of 12:20:28. On October 25, 1958, Hopcroft, of Ealing, and a member of Thames Valley Harriers, decided to run in the opposite direction from the traditional direction from London to Box, and set off from Hyde Park Corner at 5 a.m.

Hopcroft wrote, "I had always regarded 5 a.m. as the most unearthly hour and swore that, once I left the army, nothing would ever get me up at this time, but there I was at Hyde Park Corner, all ready to run 100 miles to the little village of Box. A foggy morning, but not too cold, and at 5 a.m. precisely, we were away. We being three, **John Legge**, **Bill Wortley** and myself."

At mile five, Hopcroft parted company with the other runners and went on ahead for the rest of the journey alone, battling the clock. He reached the marathon mark in 3:02.

He reached 30 miles at Reading in under three and a half hours before the hills started. Crowds cheered him on, and he reached 50 miles in 5:46:37. "Between 60 and 70 miles, I had my first feed, a cup of tomato soup and a very thin savoury sandwich of whole-meal bread dipped in soup. I gobbled it down as quickly as possible while half trotting. At 80 miles (9:36:26) I was really in trouble. For the first time, I had two or three little walks, 20 yards or so. Another wash, with my attendants pulling the bucket away from me just as I was enjoying it. Another meal as before and I was away to a really good spell of eight miles at a speed just inside seven-minute miles."

At mile 95, he was told by a young local cyclist that he was going up his last hill. He had exactly 48 minutes left to beat the record. He said, "By now we had a terrific following of motorists, motor and pedal cyclists and pedestrians running." Large groups of spectators cheered as they were told that a world record was being broken.

"Only three miles left now. But what is this? Another hill, and this proved to be the last straw. I just couldn't run up it. Pleadings and exhortations almost turned to threats in an effort to keep me running." His crew chief drove to the finish and then ran toward him, bringing their last bottle of pop, which he gulped. He also received the welcome news that after the next group of trees, that it was all downhill.

"It was dusk now and what a joy to see the lights in the village of Box, but where was the Bear Inn? Just around the corner. To my relief, I saw a big banner across the road with the wonder word 'finish.'" He finished in a new world record  on the course of 12:18:16 and said, "What a reception there was. Almost the whole village had turned out. A garland of flowers round my neck and females queuing to congratulate me in the traditional manner."

1959 100-mile Race in Surrey, England

The Road Runners Club organized a 100-mile race in 1959, hoping to beat Hopcroft's 100-mile world record of 12:18:16. The event was called, "Walton-on-Thames 100 Mile Road Race."

On October 24, 1959, at 4 a.m., twelve men set out to run twenty times around a five-mile circuit at Walton-on-

Thames, Surrey, England. Race Director **Ernest Neville** said, "The ambition of a lot of athletes is to say they have run 100 miles, and this is their chance to do it."

"Good progress was made in the calm conditions. At 30 miles, there were five runners bunched together in the lead. They were all running steadily and keeping within scheduled time, two minutes ahead of the world record." **Reg Minchington** (1928-) reached the 50-mile mark first in 6:00:14 followed by **Arthur Mail**, with 6:01:37. Minchington withdrew with back trouble at mile 55 and Mail took the lead.

Arthur Mail, (1922-) age 37, of Derby, England, won in 13:17:39,

Arthur Mail

Don Turner finished second with 13:33:54, and **Ken Parsons** in third with 17:22:40. The others did not finish, including Hopcroft. Mail said, "I must be crazy to run 100 miles." It was his first and only time competing 100 miles.

Jackie Mekler Tries to Beat Hopcoft's Record

Jack "Jackie Mekler" (1932-2019), was yet another amazing ultrarunner from South Africa who also was a five-time winner of the Comrades Marathon. His first Comrades attempt was in 1952. In 1953 he ran in Hayward's Box to London 100 miler at the young age of 21. Mekler finished second to Hayward (12:20:28) with a time of 13:08:06, which also beat the old world record. In 1954 he broke the 50-mile world record with 5:24:27.

In 1958, Mekler decided to try to beat Hayward's road 100-mile world record. Hayward believed Mekler could do it comfortably. Mekler did not want to do it in a solo attempt and asked that a race be organized. A sea-level course was found, but due to lack of support and Mekler's poor condition at the time, the idea was scrapped and soon Hopcroft beat him to it, breaking Haward's 100-mile world record later that year.

After winning London to Brighton in 1960 with a course record of 5:25:56, just three weeks later, Mekler decided to attempt breaking Hopcroft's 100-mile record on Bath Road, going from Hyde Park Corner to Box. He knew that going after records in England was better than in South Africa because of the lower altitude.

The solo run organized by the Orad Runners' Club started at 4 a.m. on October 16, 1960. The unconventional reverse direction from London was necessary to avoid heavy London traffic in the late afternoon. Ultrarunning legend, **Peter Gavuzzi,** gave him a pre-race massage and Hopcroft, paced Mekler for the first 10 miles out of London. He said, "I appreciated this sporting, kind and encouraging gesture from the record holder."

A cold wind blew an icy blast on Mekler's exposed legs, and it seemed impossible for him to warm up. At 17 miles, he was only two minutes behind record pace. "I knew I was not running as freely or as easily as I had hoped." He had his first drink there, bottled lemon squash with glucose and salt. He went on and hit the marathon mark in 3:04, still just two minutes behind the record pace.

"The wind and weather remained cruel. As the darkness of night gave way to the cold, the first hint of trouble occurred in a pain behind my right knee. I continued to run into a strong and icy headwind, and my running lacked ease and confidence." By mile 40 he realized that his chance of setting a record was slipping away, ten minutes behind Hopcroft's pace. He reached 50 miles in 6:08:06 with a painful knee and swollen Achilles tendon. At that point, he quit in great disappointment. "I felt that I had been cheated as I was still full of pent-up energy and enthusiasm, but once again disaster had struck."

Mekler's Achilles injury was serious and in those days was regarded as untreatable and career-ending. But in 1961, a successful surgery was performed and in 1962, he had completely healed and was winning races again. **Jackie Mekler** never raced 100 miles again but completed an impressive running career. He died in Cape Town, South Africa, on July 1, 2019, at the age of 87.

Ron Hopcroft continued to compete at ultra distances until 1961 after being stopped by an ankle injury and the pressure of business and family commitments. But he served many years as president of running clubs and volunteered at many track and cross-country events until 2007. He died at the age of 98 in 2016.

100-Mile World Record Progression

100-Mile World Record Progression - Amateur and Professional - All Surfaces (1762-1960) - Men				
Time	Name	Country	Year	Place
23:15:00	John Hague	Great Britain	1762	England
21:20:00	Foster Powell	Great Britain	1788	Bath Road, Eng
20:35:00	Wills	Great Britain	1789	
19:00:00	Robert Barclay Allardice	Great Britain	1806	Ury, Scotland
19:00:00	William Cross	Great Britain	1806	Ury, Scotland
17:52:00	Edward Rayner	Great Britain	1824	Biddenden, England
17:03:06	George Hazael	Great Britain	1878	London, Eng
15:35:31	George Hazael	Great Britain	1879	London, Eng
13:57:13	Charles Rowell	Great Britain	1880	London, Eng
13:26:30	Charles Rowell	Great Britain	1882	New York City, NY
13:21:19	Hardy Ballington	South Africa	1927	Bath Road, Eng
12:20:28	Wally Hayward	South Africa	1953	Bath Road, Eng
12:18:16	Ron Hopcroft	Great Britain	1958	Bath Road, Eng

100-Mile World Record Progression - Amateur and Professional - All Surfaces (1762-1960) - Women				
Time	Name	Country	Year	Place
<24:00:00	Anne Fitzgibbons	Great Britain	1869	Oneida, NY
23:05:00	M'lle Dupree	U.S.A	1878	Mankato, MN
22:22:00	Geraldine Watson	South Africa	1934	Durban, South Africa

Sources

Chapter One

- P. S. Marshall, *King of the Peds*
- Russell Field, *Playing for Change: The Continuing Struggle for Sport and Recreation*
- Kentish Weekly Post (England), Sep 13, 1739
- The Ipswich Journal (England), Feb 25, 1758, Aug 21, 1762, Dec 30, 1876
- The Derby Mercury (England), Nov 10, 1737, Jun 5, 1761, Dec 24, 1773, Sep 26, 1777, Jun 12, 1788, Jul 9, 1789, Dec 18, 1822, Apr 21, 1824
- The Edinburgh Advertiser (Scotland), Jul 14, 1789
- The Leeds Intelligencer and Yorkshire General Advertiser (England), Apr 22, 1793
- Jackson's Oxford Journal (England), Aug 4, 1810, Aug 3, 1811
- South Eastern Gazette (Kent, England), May 14, 1816
- Cambridge Chronicle and Journal (England), May 24, 1816
- The Lancaster Gazette (England), May 25, 1816, Mar 11, 1820
- The Exeter Flying Post, Jul 3, 1817, Feb 22, 1860
- Liverpool Mercury (England), Jul 11, 1817, Apr 23, 1824
- Glasgow Herald (Scotland), Jun 24, 1822
- The Times (London, England), Aug 30, 1822
- The Bath Chronicle (England), May 29, 1823
- Berrow's Worcester Journal (England), Oct 2, 1823
- The Evening Post (New York City, New York), Jun 8, 1824
- The Bristol Mercury and Daily Post (England), Jul 18, 1825
- The Bury and Norwich Post (England), Jun 27, 1827
- The Observer (London, England), Nov 12, Dec 23, 1827
- The Yorkshire Herald (England), Nov 29, 1828
- The Susquehanna Democrat (Wilkes-Barre, Pennsylvania), Oct 30, 1829
- Bell's Life in London and Sporting Chronicle (England), Feb 14, 1830
- The Times-Picayune (New Orleans, Louisiana), Oct 24, 1837
- Public Ledger (Philadelphia, Pennsylvania), Oct 25, 1837
- The Guard (Holy Springs, Mississippi), Oct 11, 1842
- Glasgow Herald (Ireland), Jun 24, 1844
- Woolmer's Exeter and Plymouth Gazette (England), May 31, 1851
- The Era (London, England), Jun 6, 1847, Feb 26, 1860

- The Hampshire Advertiser (England), Sep 7, 1861, Jan 4, 1862
- York Herald (Yorkshire, England), Jan 26, 1867
- Sioux City Journal (Iowa), Mar 16, 1867
- The Times (London, England), Dec 13, 1867
- The Burlington Free Press (Vermont), Nov 27, 1867
- The Daily Milwaukee News (Wisconsin), Aug 31, 1867
- The Holt County Sentinel (Oregon, Missouri), Jan 10, 1868
- Arizona Miner (For Whipple, Arizona), Jan 25, 1868
- Leavenworth Daily (Kansas), Apr 8, 1868
- The Titusville Herald (Pennsylvania), Nov 26, 1867
- Raftsman's Journal (Clearfield, Pennsylvania), Apr 22, 1868
- Star Tribune (Minneapolis, Minnesota), Apr 23, 1868
- The Philadelphia Inquirer (Pennsylvania), Jul 27, 1868
- The Louisville Daily Courier (Kentucky), Jul 6, 1868
- New York Daily Herald, May 22, 1870
- The Sun (New York, New York), May 28, 1870
- Wayne Country Herald (Pennsylvania), Dec 15, 1870
- Buffalo Morning Express (New York), Sep 29, 1879
- Buffalo Courier (New York), Oct 12, 1868, Mar 15, 1869
- Chicago Tribune (Illinois), Apr 8, 1869
- The New North-West (Deer Lodge, Montana), Apr 13, 1872
- The Brooklyn Daily Eagle, Oct 27, 1868
- The Tennessean (Nashville), Nov 15, 1868
- The Brooklyn Daily Eagle (New York), Nov, 20, 1868, Dec 15, 1868
- Buffalo Evening Post (New York), Apr 21, 1869
- The Atlanta Constitution (Georgia), Oct 22, 1871
- Wisconsin State Journal (Madison, Wisconsin), Dec 5, 1873
- The Rutland Daily Globe (Vermont), Mar 5, 1875

Chapters Two and Three

- P. S. Marshall, *King of the Peds*
- Matthew Algeo, *Pedestrianism: When Watching People Walk Was America's Favorite Spectator Sport*
- Andy Milroy, *Long Distance Record Book*
- P. S. Marshall, "George Hazael: The First Man to Run 600 Miles in 6 Days!"
- Harry Hall, *The Pedestriennes: America's Forgotten Superstars*
- Rob Hadgraft, *Pioneers in Bloomer: The Intrepid Pedestriennes – British Sport's First Female Celebrities*

- The Philadelphia Inquirer (Pennsylvania), Sept 2, 1868
- *Mark Twain's Letters, Volume 6: 1874-1875*
- The Indiana Progress (Indiana, Pennsylvania), May 8, 1873
- Chicago Tribune (Illinois), Jul 14, Aug 22-23, Oct 8, 1874, May 30, 1875, Oct 17, 1875, Dec 24, 1876
- The Coshocton Democrat (Ohio), Jan 6, 1874
- The Findlay Jeffersonian (Ohio), November 27, 1874
- The South Bend Tribune (Indiana), Apr 12, 1875
- The St. Albans Advertiser (Vermont), May 21, 1875
- Intelligencer Journal (Lancaster, Pennsylvania), May 18, 1875
- The Philadelphia Inquirer (Pennsylvania), May 31, 1875
- The Brooklyn Daily Eagle (New York), Jun 21, 1875
- Boston Post (Massachusetts), May 24, 1875
- Time Union (Brooklyn, New York), Aug 14, 1875
- The St. Albans Advertiser (Vermont), May 21, 1875
- Harrisburg Telegraph (Pennsylvania), Oct 23, 1875
- The Indianapolis News (Indiana), May 3, 1875
- Lebanon Daily News (Pennsylvania), May 4, 1875
- The Age (Melbourne, Australia), Jul 20, 1875
- The Topeka Weekly Times (Kansas), Dec 10, 1875
- Northern Echo (Dalington, Durham, England), Feb 17, 1876
- Daily News (London, England), Feb 18, 1876
- Reynold's Newspaper (London, England), Feb 13, 26-27 1876
- The Era (London, England), Feb 6, 1876
- The Nottinghamshire Guardian (England), Feb 11, 1876
- The Huddersfield Chronicle (England), Feb 28, 1876
- The Star (Saint Peter Port, England), May 3, 1877
- The Inter Ocean (Chicago, Illinois), Nov 6, 1877
- The Leavenworth Press (Kansas), Nov 10, 1877
- The Buffalo Sunday Morning News (New York), Nov 11, 1877
- The Ottawa Free Trader (Illinois), Jun 23, 1877
- The Standard (London, England), Oct 29, 1878
- The Morning Post (London, England), Mar 7, 1876
- The Times-Democrat (New Orleans, Louisiana), Dec 26, 1875
- The Daily Milwaukee News (Wisconsin), Feb 6, 1876
- Pittsburgh Daily Post (Pennsylvania), Feb 7, 1876
- The Boston Globe (Boston, Massachusetts), Oct 27, Dec 25, 1876, Feb 10, 28, 1877
- The Columbus Republican (Indiana), Nov 9, 1876
- Vermont Journal (Windsor, Vermont), Dec 2, 1876

- Kansas Weekly Herald (Hiawatha, Kansas), Feb 14, 1878
- The Intelligencer (Anderson, South Carolina), Sep 13, 1877
- North Wales Chronicle (Bangor, Wales), Dec 1, 1877
- The York Dispatch (York, Pennsylvania), Aug 15, 1877
- The Rock Island Argus (Illinois), Jun 2, 1877
- The Burlington Free Press (Burlington, Vermont), Aug 24, 1877
- The Saint Paul Globe (Minnesota), Sep 5, 1878
- The Star Tribune (Minneapolis, Minnesota), Jul 1, 3, 5, 22 1878
- The Daily Milwaukee News (Wisconsin), Jul 14, 1878
- Des Moines Register (Iowa), Oct 30, Nov 13, 1878
- Kansas Daily Tribune (Lawrence, Kansas), Feb 8, 1879
- Fitchburg Sentinel (Massachusetts), Mar 7, 1877
- The Sacramento Bee (California), Jul 6, 1878
- The San Francisco Examiner (California), Aug 5, 1878
- Los Angeles Herald (California), Aug 21, 1878
- The South Bend Tribune (Indiana), Dec 21,23, 1878
- The Cincinnati Daily Star (Ohio), May 30, 1878
- Buffalo Weekly Courier (New York), Sep 11, 1878
- The Belvidere Standard (Illinois), Dec 17, 1878
- Email from May Marshall's great-great-grandson on July 13, 2021

Chapters Four and Five

- P. S. Marshall "Charlie Rowell – aka the Cambridge Wonder"
- P. S. Marshall, "George Hazael: The First Man to Run 600 Miles in 6 Days!"
- P. S. Marshall, *King of the Peds*
- Matthew Algeo, *Pedestrianism: When Watching People Walk Was America's Favorite Spectator Sport*
- Andy Milroy, *Long Distance Record Book*
- Harry Hall, *The Pedestriennes: America's Forgotten Superstars*
- The Western Spirit (Paola, Kansas), May 1, 1874
- The Brooklyn Sunday Sun (New York), May 17, 1874
- The Luzerne Union (Wilkes-Barre, Pennsylvania), Sep 23, 1874
- The United Opinion (Bradford, Vermont), Oct 3, 1874
- Matawan Journal (New Jersey), Dec 5, 1874
- The Valley Sentinel (Carlisle, Pennsylvania), Aug 30, 1878
- Rutland Daily Herald (Vermont), Feb 12, 14, Apr 25, 1879
- Reading Times (Pennsylvania), Jan 23, 1879

- The Boston Globe, (Massachusetts), Jun 30, 1878, Feb 8, Apr 18-20, May 19, 1879
- The Muscatine Journal (Iowa), Oct 11, 1879
- The Lake Geneva Herald (Wisconsin), Feb 8, 1879
- The Morning Democrat (Davenport, Iowa), Apr 17, 1879
- The Saint Paul Globe (Minnesota), Apr 7, 1880
- Fayette County Herald (Washington, Ohio), Jul 3, 17, 1879
- Public Ledger (Memphis, Tennessee), Feb 27, 1879
- Chicago Tribune (Illinois), Mar 15, 1879
- The Sun (New York, New York), Apr 27, 1879
- The York Daily (Pennsylvania), Dec 29, 1879, Jan 2, 1880
- The Atchison Daily Champion (Kansas), May 17, 1885
- The Baltimore Sun (Maryland), Mar 21, 1879
- The Daily Gazette (Wilmington, Delaware), Mar 22, 1879
- The Cincinnati Enquirer (Ohio), Mar 22, 1879
- The Muscatine Journal, (Iowa), May 12, 1879
- Nebraska State Journal (Lincoln, Nebraska), Feb 17, 1881
- The Morning Post (London, England), Apr 22, 1879, Nov 2, 1880
- The Graphic (New York, New York), Jan 27, Mar 8, 1881
- The Buffalo Commercial (New York), Feb 4, 1882
- The Boston Globe (Massachusetts), Feb 23, 1882
- Buffalo Evening News (New York), Feb 27, 1882
- New York Tribune (New York), Feb 27, 1882
- The New York Times (New York), Feb 28, 1882, Feb 7, 1888
- The Bismarck Tribune (North Dakota), May 9, 1884
- The Argentine Eagle (Kansas), Aug 26, 1892
- Abilene Weekly Reflector (Kansas), Jul 16, 1896
- Evening Star (Washington D.C.), Dec 26, 1896
- The Gazette (Montreal, Canada), Dec 28, 1896
- The Ottawa Journal (Ontario, Canada), Jul 19, 1897

Chapters Six and Ten

- Buffalo Morning Express (New York), Jul 11, 1878
- The Winnipeg Tribune (Canada), Feb 13, 1899
- The Inter Ocean (Chicago, Illinois), Aug 21, 1904, Dec 8, 1905, Sep 3, 1906, Oct 23, 25 1907, Apr 29, Jun 12, 1908, Oct 4, 1908, Jul 25, 1909
- The Daily Review (Decatur, Illinois), Aug 31, 1904
- The Perry Daily Chief (Iowa), Aug 17, 1905
- The Pittsburgh Press (Pennsylvania), Aug 17, 1905

- The Minneapolis Journal (Minnesota), Dec 8, 1905
- The Oshkosh Northwestern (Wisconsin), Dec 8, 1905
- Chicago Tribune (Illinois), May 6, Aug 21, 1906, Jan 3, Jul 20, 25 1909, Oct 16, 19, Nov 5, 1916, May 18, 1917, Oct 22, 1918
- The Oklahoma Post (Oklahoma), Aug 25, 1906
- The Journal Times (Racine, Wisconsin), Sep 1, 4, 1906, Oct 18, 1907, Dec 8, 1917
- The Minneapolis Journal (Minnesota), Sep 4, 1906
- The Buffalo Commercial (New York), Nov 1, 1906
- The San Francisco Examiner (California), Oct 25, 1907, Feb 17-18, 21, 27-28, Apr 2, 1910
- Muncie Evening Press (Indian), May 27, 1909
- Lincoln Journal Star (Nebraska), Jul 23, 1909
- Nanaimo Daily News (British Columbia, Canada), Jul 19, 1909
- Fort Wayne Daily News (Indiana), Jul 24, 1909
- The La Crosse Tribune (Wisconsin), Jul 24, 1909
- The Leavenworth Times (Kansas), Jul 24, 1909
- Times Union (Brooklyn, New York), Jul 26, 1909
- San Francisco Chronicle (California), Feb 26, 1910
- Reno Gazette-Journal (Nevada), Feb 28, 1910
- Rutland Daily Herald (Vermont), Aug 18, 1911
- Louis Star and Times (Missouri), Oct 9, 1916
- The Indianapolis News (Indiana), Oct 17-18, 1916, Jan 6, 1919
- The Brooklyn Citizen (New York), Oct 18, 1916
- The Salt Lake Herald-Republican (Salt Lake City, Utah), Oct 18, 1916
- The Pantagraph (Bloomington, Illinois), Oct 19, 1916
- The Winnipeg Tribune, Nov 22, 1916
- The Star Press (Muncie, Indiana), Nov 5, 1916
- The Allentown Leader (Pennsylvania), Dec 15, 1916
- Buffalo Evening News (New York), Dec 16, 1916
- The Dispatch (Moline, Illinois), Feb 23, 1917
- The Times (Munster, Indiana), Mar 24, 1917
- The Ithaca Journal (New York), Apr 19, 1917
- Joseph Gazette (Missouri), Jun 6, 1917
- The Daily Review (Decatur, Illinois), Jun 1, 1917
- Louis Post-Dispatch (Missouri), Jun 2, 1917
- The Rock Island Argus (Illinois), May 28, 1919
- The Province (Vancouver, Canada), Sep 18, 1927
- Palladium-Item (Richmond, Indiana), Jun 20, 1929
- The San Francisco Examiner (California), Jun 21, 23, 1929

- The Vancouver Sun (Canada), Sep 10, 1929
- Gallup Journal (New Mexico), Jul 26, 2013

Chapter Seven

- 150th Anniversary of the First London to Brighton Bike Ride
- The London to Brighton Bike Ride
- History of the London to Brighton
- Sandra Brown, *Unbroken Contact: One Hundred Years of Walking with Surrey Walking Club*
- Belfast News-Letter (Northern, Ireland), Mar 16-1869
- Charles G. Harper, *The Brighton Road: The Classic Highway to the South*
- The Pittsburgh Press (Pennsylvania), Nov 23, 1902
- The Times (London, England), Nov 1, 1902, Sep 14, 1908
- The Gazette (Montreal, Canada), Dec 1, 1902
- The Fall River Daily Herald (Massachusetts), Dec 1, 1902
- The Guardian (London, England), May 2, 1903, Jun 5, 1903, Jun 24, 1907, Sep 14, 1908, Jun 21, 1926, Jun 22, 24, 1929
- The Sun (New York City), July 21, 1907
- The Observer (London, England), Jun 23, 1907, Sep 19, 1909, Sep 1, 1912, Jun 23, 1929
- 1908 Thomas Hammond, the Record Walker
- Surrey Walking Club Gazette (No, 3, Vol I, 1908)
- E. (Tommy) Hammond, "World's Best"
- The Gazette (Montreal, Canada), Sep 6, 1909, Jul 5, 1912, Jul 16, 1921
- The Centurions Walking Club
- Centurions History
- List of British Centurions 1911
- Surrey Walking Club Handbook
- Stock Exchange Athletic Club History
- The Illustrated Sporting and Dramatic News, Jun 29, 1907
- Tom Payne – Walker and Musician Extraordinaire
- Tom Payne: The World-Famous Musician-Athlete
- 79th Walk London to Brighton Centenary Race
- The Boston Globe (Massachusetts), Aug 3, 1914
- The Province (Vancouver, Canada), Sep 15, 1929

Chapter Eight

- Arthur Newton, *Running in Three Continents*

- Rob Hadgraft, *Tea with Mr. Newton: 100,000 Miles – The Longest 'Protest March' in History*
- Mark Whitaker, *Running for their Lives: The Extraordinary Story of Britain's Greatest Ever Distance Runners*
- Comrades Marathon results
- Ian Champion, *Arthur Newton's 100-mile Road Running Record*
- John Cameron-Dow. *Comrades Marathon: The Ultimate Human Race*
- The Guardian (London, England), Oct 4, 1924, Oct 4, 1924, Dec 10, 1927
- The Boston Globe (Massachusetts), Nov 15, 1924
- The Bridgeport Telegram (Connecticut), Jul 12, 1927
- Hartford Courant (Connecticut), Aug 16, 1927
- The Spokesman-Review (Spokane, Washington), Mar 20, 1925
- The Province (Vancouver, Canada), Apr 6, 1931
- The Iola Register (Kansas), Jan 17, 1934
- Sioux City Journal (Iowa), Mar 4, 1934
- The Windsor Star (Ontario, Canada), Aug 17, 1934
- The Gazette (Montreal, Quebec, Canada), Sep 8, 1959

Chapter Nine

- David Blaikie, "The history of the London to Brighton Race"
- Rob Hadgraf, *Tea with Mr Newton: 100,000 Miles - The Longest 'Protest March' in History*
- Andy Milroy, "Hardy Ballington – The Forgotten Great Ultrarunner"
- John Cameron-Dow, *Comrades Marathon - The Ultimate Human Race*
- Albuquerque Journal (New Mexico), Oct 10, 1929
- Morristown Gazette Mail (Tennessee), Jul 2, 1930
- The Windsor Star (Windsor, Ontario, Canada), Dec 30, 1933
- The Albion Argus (Nebraska) Mar 22, 1934
- The Tennessean (Nashville, Tennessee), May 23, 1937
- The Observer (London, England), May 23, 1937
- The Boston Globe (Massachusetts), Jul 21, 1937
- Star-Gazette (Elmira, New York), Jul 18, 1938
- Press and Sun Bulletin (Binghamton, New York), Aug 3, 1938
- The News and Observer (Raleigh, North Carolina), Jun 17, 1940
- The Kansas City Star (Missouri), Jan 30, Jun 1,20, Aug 3, 1941
- Lancaster New Era (Pennsylvania), Jan 30, 1941
- Arizona Republic (Phoenix, Arizona), Feb 4, 1941
- The Times (Shreveport Louisiana), Feb 8, 1941

- The St. Louis Star and Times (Missouri), Sep 22, 1941
- The Jackson Sun (Jackson, Tennessee), Jul 21, 1941
- Wilkes-Barre Times Leader (Pennsylvania), Jul 21, 1941
- The Kansas City Times (Missouri), Jun 27, Jul 11,21, Sep 22, 1941
- The Age (Melbourne, Australia), Aug 1, 1942
- The Cushing Daily Citizen (Oklahoma), Aug 19, 1942
- The Amarillo Globe-Times (Texas), Jan 27, 1943
- The Gettysburg Times (Pennsylvania), Jun 2, 1943
- The Miami News (Florida), Jun 3, 1943
- The Evening Times (Sayre, Pennsylvania), Oct 13, 1943
- Louis Post-Dispatch (Missouri), Mar 11, 1944
- Dayton Daily News (Ohio), Sep 24, 1944
- The Bangor Daily News (Maine), Aug 15, 1944
- The Gazette (Cedar Rapids, Iowa), Apr 19, 1945
- The Knoxville Journal (Tennessee), Nov 25, 1945
- The Daily Reporter (Greenfield, Indiana), Dec 15, 1945
- The Ithaca Journal (New York), Aug 27, 1935, Aug 2-5, 1938, Nov 26, 1945, Sep 17, 1946, May 27, 1947, Jan 12, 1950
- Democrat and Chronicle (Rochester, New York), Jul 2, 1947
- The Tipton Daily Tribune (Indiana), Aug 30, 1957
- The Sydney Morning Herald (Australia), Mar 18, 1966

Chapters Eleven and Fifteen

- M. Jamieson, Wally Hayward, *Just Call me Wally*
- Jackie Mekler, *Running Alone: The autobiography of long-distance runner Jackie Mekler*
- John Cameron-Dow, *Comrades Marathon - The Ultimate Human Race*
- "Ron Hopcoft" Thames Valley Harriers
- Ron Hopcoft 100-mile race report
- The Times (Shreveport, Louisiana), Jun 27, 1950
- Valley Times (North Hollywood, California), Jan 20, 1951
- Statesman Journal (Salem, Oregon), Jun21, Jull 3, Aug 2, 1951, Sep 1, 1952, Jul 12, 1961, Apr 30, 1962
- Greater Oregon (Albany, Oregon), Jul 20, 1951
- Albany Democrat-Herald (Albany, Oregon), Jul 19, 1951
- Alabama Journal (Montgomery, Alabama), Nov 23, 1951
- The Vancouver News-Herald (Canada), Nov 23, 1953
- The Miami News (Florida), Nov 21, 1953
- The San Francisco Examiner (California), Nov 23, 1951, Nov 22, 1953

- Coventry Evening Telegraph (England), Sep 26, Oct 24, Nov 21, 1953, Jan 27, 1954, Oct 17, 24 1959
- Shields Daily News (England), Nov 23, 1953
- Aberdeen Evening Express (England), Nov 23, 1953, Oct 15, 1960
- The Daily Chronicle (De Kalb, Illinois), Jan 31, 1955
- The Daily Register (Harrisburg, Illinois), Jan 24, 1955
- Sunday News (Lancaster, Pennsylvania), Feb 20, 1955
- The Morning News (Wilmington, Delaware), Aug 15, 1957
- The Observer (London, England), Jul 7, 1957, Oct 25, 1959
- The Courier-News (Bridgewater, New Jersey), Mar 31, 1958
- Leicester Evening Mail (England), Jul 19, 1958
- Skegness News (England), Jul 23, 1958
- The Ottawa Citizen (Canada), Oct 4, 1958
- The Stafford and Med Staffs Newsletter (England), Dec 12, 1959
- Liverpool Echo (England), Jul 19, 1958
- Hammersmith & Shepherds Bush Gazette (England), Oct 31, 1958
- Rutland Daily Herald (Vermont), Oct 2, 1959
- The Daily Oklahoman (Oklahoma City, Oklahoma), Oct 25, 1959
- The People (England), Oct 25, 1959
- The Hanford Sentinel (California), Feb 19, 1960
- The Monitor (McAllen, Texas), Feb 19, 1960
- Press and Sun Bulletin (Binghamton, New York), Feb 19, 1960
- The Logansport Press (Indiana), Feb 20, 1960
- The Spokesman-Review (Spokane, Washington), Feb 20, 1960
- The Morning News (Wilmington, Delaware), Feb 20, 1960
- The Press Democrat (Santa Rosa, California), Feb 21, 1960
- Great Falls Tribune (Montana), Feb 21, 1960
- Herald and Review (Decatur, Illinois), Sep 24, 1960
- The Decatur Daily Review (Illinois), Sep 25, 1960

Chapter Twelve

- Pittsburgh Press, Jan 31, 1909, May 10, 1914, Mar 24, 1915, Oct 7, 1931, Sep 30, 1940, May 12, 14, 1944, May 12, 1946, Aug 21, 1949, Apr 11, 1965, Aug 15, 1949, Jul 3, 1961, May 6, 1967
- Pittsburgh Post-Gazette, Oct 26, 1917, May 24, 1943, Sept 24, 1945, 15 Aug 1949, Aug 28, 1950, Sep 9, 1958, 21 May 1960, Jul 4, 1961, Sept 5, 1961, May 7, 1962
- Pittsburgh Sun-Telegraph, Jul 25, 1936, Jun 6, 1939, Jul 20, 1941
- South Bend News-Times, Nov 7, 1914, Dec 11, 1914

- New Castle News, 27, Oct 1915, June 7, 1916, 19 Aug 1930
- The Evening News (Harrisburg, Pennsylvania), Aug 22, 1930
- The Indiana Gazette, Sep 24, 1945
- Pittsburgh Daily Post, Dec 4, 1916
- The Morning News (Wilmington, Deleware), Aug 7, 1929
- Nebraska State Journal, Oct 4, 1945

Chapter Thirteen

- Numerous news articles from The Corpus Christi Caller-Times, 1953-1958.
- The Brownsville Herald, Mar 19, 1953, May 6, 1955
- The Monitor (McAllen, Texas), Mar 30 1953, May 8, 1955, Aug 1, 1965
- Lubbock Avalanche-Journal, Mar 29, 1953
- The eagle (Bryan Texas), May 9, 1955
- Victoria Advocate (Victoria, Texas), May 10, 1955, 10 May 1958.
- Abilene Reporter, Jun 4, 1956
- Waco Tribune-Herald, May 25, 1958

Chapter Fourteen

- John D. Barton, *A History of Duchesne County*.
- Edward S. Sears, *Running Through the Ages*
- Andy Milroy, *North American Ultrarunning: A History*
- Geoff Williams, *C. C. Pyle's Amazing Foot Race: The True Story of the 1928 Coast-to-Coast Run Across America*
- The Ipswich Journal (England), Nov 7, 1818
- Burlington Weekly Hawk-Eye, Sep 9, 1880
- Chicago Tribune, Oct 16, 1879, Sept 15, 1880
- The Philadelphia Inquirer, Oct 3, 1957
- The Daily Tribune (Wisconsin), Nov 5, 1957
- The Uintah Basin Standard, Nov 7,21, 1957, Jul 24, 31, 1958
- The News-Review (Oregon), Nov 16, 1957
- The Daily Herald (Provo, Utah), Nov 15, 17-18, 1957, Mar 4, 1958
- Bennington Banner (Vermont), Nov 18, 1957
- The Salt Lake Tribune, Jan 20, 1958, Apr 15, 1958, July 23, 1958
- Lehi Free Press, Jul 31, 1958.
- The Times (Shreveport, Louisiana), Jul 23, 1958
- Great Falls Tribune, Jun 9, 1960
- The Daily Inter Lake (Kalispell, Montana), Jun 17, 1960

- The Gazette (Montreal, Canada), Dec 23, 1936
- Democrat and Chronicle (Rochester, New York), Dec 29, 1936
- The Amarillo Globe-Times, Jul 4, 1950
- The Salt Lake Tribune, Mar 28, 1943
- Casper Star-Tribune, Jul 24, 1958
- The Bee (Danville, Virginia) Sep 28, 1927
- Rocky Mount Telegram (Rocky Mount, North Carolina), Jul 23, 1958
- Tara Parker-Pope, "The Human Body is Built for Distance," The New York Times, Oct 26, 2009
- Arizona Republic, April 6, 1984, April 29, 1985
- Albany Democrat-Herald (Oregon), Jul 25, 1849

About the Author

David "Davy" R. Crockett is a veteran ultrarunner and historian. He began serious running in 2004 and finished more than one hundred 100-mile races during the next fourteen years. In 2005, he combined his love for running and history by organizing the "Pony Express Trail 50 and 100" held on the historic Pony Express Trail in the west desert of Utah.

In 2018, he established ultrarunninghistory.com and the Ultrarunning History Podcast, authoring long articles and episodes every two weeks, documenting long-forgotten stories of the sport.

In 2020, he became the new Director of the American Ultrarunning Hall of Fame, which is hosted on ultrarunninghistory.com.

Davy Crockett is the author of four previous books on the American 19th-century westward migration, and three previous books in the Ultrarunning History Series, *Frank Hart: The First Black Ultrarunning Star, Grand Canyon Rim to Rim History, and Strange Running Tales: When Ultrarunning was a Reality Show*. He has also published numerous articles in magazines and newspapers, and two online books on ultrarunning.

He and his wife Linda are the parents of six children and twelve grandchildren, all living in Utah.

Ultrarunninghistory.com

Crockettclan.org/blog

Index

Made in the USA
Columbia, SC
26 November 2023

27162336R00137